How to Self-publish and Market a Book

A comprehensive guide to an integrated approach to self-publishing and marketing a book

By Hank Quense

Reviews for Creating Stories:

Joylene Butler: Author of Matowak Women Who Cries:
This book is a true treasure and needs to be in the library of every writer worldwide.

Indie Reader:
CREATING STORIES is a useful resource for new writers who have a terrific story idea but aren't sure how to go about turning that into a functional, readable, enjoyable novel

Mark Henderson: British author of Cruel and Unusual Punnishments
Hank doesn't purport to tell reader how to produce creative ideas, but offers guidance on how to turn those ideas into readable fiction.
I recommend Creating Stories unreservedly to fiction writers everywhere.

© 2019 Hank Quense
All Rights Reserved

License Notes

This book is licensed for your personal use only. This book may not be re-sold or given away to other people. If you would like to share this book with another person, please purchase an additional copy for each recipient. If you're reading this book and did not purchase it, or it was not purchased for your use only, then please return it and purchase your own copy. Thank you for respecting the hard work of this author.

ISBN:

978-1733342414

Published in the United States of America.

Published by Strange Worlds Publishing

Acknowledgements

This book owes a debt of gratitude to a plucky street team who took my typo-filled early drafts and told me what I had wrong and what I had to explain better.

Here is a list of these writers and authors:

Elaine Durbach

Mark Lance

Jordan Lewis

Anna Faversham

Barbara Mealer

Aaron Rath

John Tissandier

Dale Lehman

A.J. Watson

The manuscript was edited by Bonnie Smiler. Gary Tenuta made the cover.

Table of Contents

Foreword

Chapter 1: Getting Started

Chapter 2: 6 Months Before Launch

Chapter 3: 5 Months Before Launch

Chapter 4: 4 Months Before Launch

Chapter 5: 3 Months Before Launch

Chapter 6: 2 Months Before Launch

Chapter 7: Launch

Chapter 8: Post-launch

Chapter 9: Your Book Company

Chapter 10: Additional Resources

About the Author

Foreword

Successfully self-publishing a book provides an author with a great feeling. The premise behind this book is that you have decided to self-publish a book. The project can result in an ebook only, a print book only or both ebook and print. It may not be apparent to you at this point, but ebooks and print books have different publishing procedures. This book will explain all these differences and guide you through the preparation and launch of the different editions. A piece of advice: take a deep breath and follow the step-by-step process. Many tasks are easy to accomplish and some will take time and effort. I will guide you every step of the way and separate the more challenging tasks into smaller chunks to ensure you can do it with ease. There are times when you'll be doing very little work: instead you'll be waiting for beta readers to comment on the book or for an editor to mark up your manuscript. These two tasks can easily consume two to three months, hence the need for a realistic project interval. This interval spreads out the work load and limits the number of tasks that have to be done all at once. This will ease any stress you may be feeling. If you were to sell your book to a publisher, they would take care of all (or almost all) of the publishing tasks detailed in this book, but you will still be to some degree responsible for part of the marketing. Even if you have a publisher, reading through the publishing tasks in this book will give you a much better understanding of the publishing process. This will enable you to talk more meaningfully to the publisher and that is to your advantage.

Self-publishing a book for the first time isn't for the faint of heart: it's a daunting project that takes time and money. Just because you wrote a book (of which you should be proud) doesn't mean you know anything about self-publishing that book. Authoring a book and publishing that book are two completely different endeavors.

As you start your journey toward self-publishing your book, you will undoubtedly explore the internet searching for information. That's where the trouble and confusion can start. The internet has tons of information on self-publishing. Some of this information may be accurate and some of it may be inaccurate. Some of it is wrong and some of it may lead you into the clutches of scammers and others out to make money without giving value for your money.

The best way to go about your maiden self-publishing project is to have a mentor — someone who has navigated the self-publishing swamp and survived the journey — and that is what I offer with this book. My book provides you with a wealth of information about self-publishing (indeed it lays out a plan for you to follow). I have self-published over twenty-five books, both fiction and non-fiction. Along the way, I've made mistakes and I've fallen for scams. This of course means I have a lot of experience and expertise, all of which I share.

This book recommends starting the project six months before the launch date. While this may seem strange, it provides time to complete all the tasks without going into overload. There are tasks to be completed at monthly intervals — six, five, four, three, launch and post-launch.

If you wish to shorten the project time to five months, I suggest you combine months six and five tasks which are found in Chapters 2 and 3. If you have only four months, combine months six and five as before and combine the tasks found in months four and three found in Chapters 4 and

5.

I don't recommend make it shorter than five months because of your dependency on others to finish tasks such as editing.

This book has a number of tasks for you to work on. At the end of Chapter 10, there is a detailed list of tasks organized by chapter.

Before you begin your journey into publishing and marketing, let me give you a few words of advice and encouragement: *You can do this!*

Chapter One: Getting Started

Overview

Most books on publishing deal with publishing by itself. Most books on marketing deal with marketing as a stand-alone project. I think this is the wrong approach. Self-publishing and book marketing have to be considered as an integrated project. That is what this book does; it treats publishing and marketing together as a unified project.

Successfully self-publishing a book gives one a fantastic ego boost. It's almost as good as writing the book! The thing is, self-publishing your book the professional way involves time and money (unless you elect to do it the lazy way). Technology and changes in the publishing industry have made self-publishing a book the lazy way easy to do. Indeed, it's perhaps too easy This book covers in depth the professional way.

So what is the lazy way?

In the lazy way, you finish a new draft of the manuscript on Sunday. On Monday, you buy an inexpensive generic cover, or make one yourself. On Tuesday, you upload the manuscript file and the cover file. On Wednesday, you celebrate because you are now a published author.

Let me make three comments about self-publishing the lazy way. First, the book is a piece of crap: no one will buy it or read it. Second, books that are published the lazy way are the reason self-publishing has such a bad reputation and third, authors who self-publish this way have no concept of what self-publishing means.

What self-publishing means is that you, the author, do *ALL* the work a publisher would have done if you sold the book to a publisher. This means,

among other tasks, making sure you have:
- Obtained or created a unique cover
- Enlisted the services of a professional editor
- Ensured the ebook edition conforms to the Epub3 standard
- Developed and maintained a consistent layout
- Finished other related tasks

Completing all these tasks takes time, effort and money.

Self-publishing a book the professional way means producing a quality book package to hold your quality content. The term 'quality book package' will be the theme of the publishing portion of this book.

The bulk of the work in this project will occur later on in the project. The interval from two months before launch until the magic date will be especially busy.

If you're ready to self-publish your book the right way, let's get started.

Remember: *You can do this!*

In this chapter, we'll cover the following topics:
- What type of book?
- Comparison list: ebook and print book
- Book titles
- Book publishing
- Epub3 Standard
- Book marketing
- Budgeting
- Publishing budget
- Marketing budget
- What's next?

What Type of Book?

One of the early decisions a self-publishing author has to make concerns what type of book will be published. Ebook? Print book? Both?

Ebook formats: Ebooks come in different flavors to satisfy different e-reader devices. The primary ones today are described below.

PDF format: This file type has been around for a long time. It stands for Portable Document Format and is used to read documents on a computer monitor. Tablets and phones can now view this format file type. PDF produces a file that is almost identical to the original file that created it. The advantage of the PDF file (over a Word file, for instance) is the PDF file can't be changed while the word processor file can be altered. Modern software does allow the PDF file to be marked up (with corrections or annotations), but the original text can't be changed.

EPub format: This is the world-wide standard for ebooks. Formatting a document to be published in this format can be an exasperating experience because of the stringent standards that have been developed. Most word processors assume whatever you type into the computer will be printed, hence their default settings support printing the document. Many of these default settings violate Epub3 standards, hence the need to spend time on formatting the ebook manuscript. More on this issue later on.

Mobi format: This is the format used by Amazon for its Kindle ebooks. It doesn't have the strict requirements of the Epub format.

Other formats: There are other ebook formats, such as HTML to mention one; however, most self-publishing authors will rarely, if ever, need to use them.

Print book formats: Print books come in paperback and hardcover styles. The latter are more expensive to produce and hence will demand a higher price. Print books also come in a variety of sizes that you'll have to specify in order to have your cover match the book size. My novels all are

5.5 inches by 8.5 inches. Other possible sizes are: 6x9 and 8.5x11. There are dozens of sizes available in both US and metric measurements.

Audio books: Once your ebook or print book is completed, you have the option of having an audio book edition issued. Audio books are covered in Chapter 8.

Comparison List

As you might expect, there are a number of advantages and disadvantages in publishing one or the other type of book or both types. For that reason I compiled this comparison list. It shows the pros and cons for print books and ebooks. I'm sure there are many more bullet items that can be added under each header, but these are the major ones to my way of thinking.

Ebooks: Plus
- Less expensive covers
- Faster publication cycle
- Instant global distribution
- Instant download and availability
- No book production costs
- Author gets higher percentage of sales revenue (on a lower book price)

Ebooks: Negative
- Many readers don't like e-readers and prefer to read a print book
- Some ebook seller sites are reader-hostile in that they are difficult to navigate
- Difficult to sell at book fairs and other personal appearances
- Book prices will generally be much lower than print book prices resulting in lower revenue per sale

Print: Plus

- Can be given as gifts to family and friends
- Can be sold at book fairs etc
- Bookstore sales possible
- Library sales possible

Print: Negative

- More expensive cover
- Slower distribution
- Distribution may be restricted geographically
- More expensive production costs
- Distributor sales suck up almost all the revenue leaving little for the author
- Book store returns can be a problem

As you can see from the list, ebooks and print books do have significant differences.

Book Title

Before you get locked into a title for your book, type it into a search engine like Google or Bing and see what happens. You may be surprised!

My first novel was called *Fools Gold*, an appropriate title for the story. A month or two after it was published, I Googled it and I was shock to get a list of *Fools Gold* titles that ran for 25 pages. It showed *Fools Gold* and *Fool's Gold* as the title for movies, songs, books, rock bands, albums, TV shows, games and even other material. The reason for this plethora of *Fools Gold* items is that titles can't be copyrighted and so they are available for anyone to use and re-use.

If you do a title search and this happens with your book title you may want to reconsider the title to prevent confusion with potential readers thinking your title refers to something else, like a recording by their favorite band.

Creating a title can be an agonizing ordeal as you try to get the plot, the settings or the characters to lead you into a great title. There are tools online that can make the job easier. One such tool can be found here: https://kindlepreneur.com/free-book-title-generator-tools/

Book Publishing

Self-publishing is the process of getting your book into a form that the reading public can buy and read.

The goal for self-publishing is to produce a quality book package to hold your quality content. To achieve such a book package, you have to complete the self-publishing tasks as perfectly as possible. This involves time and money. And it just isn't your time we're talking about. Others are involved in the process and their time needs to be factored into the project.

These others are: beta readers, cover artists and editors. While they may be sympathetic to your launch date, they have their own problems and workloads. Cover artists and editors especially have other clients, and you may have to wait in queue for your project to get worked on.

Quality book packages for a print book and for an ebook are quite different. Print books are easier since what you see on your computer screen is usually what the print book will look like.

To produce a quality ebook package however, the ebook must be formatted in accordance with the Epub3 standard. What you see on your computer screen will most likely not agree with this standard. For instance, to meet the Epub3 standard, you will have to eliminate the headers, footers, page breaks and page numbers associated with the print book. In addition, you cannot indent the first line of a new paragraph by using the space bar or the tab key. This formatting effort can be tedious and it may require outside help. Hiring such an expert represents another possible interval and expense that has to be accounted for. Smashwords keeps a list of authors who will do formatting and book layouts for a fee. They are not Smashwords employees, just authors looking to pick up a few bucks: https://www.smashwords.com/list. It is also possible to deploy software. Some products or websites are: Reedsy, Upwork, Fivver and others. Most of these software products will require money to either subscribe to the site or buy the software. Before investing the money, investigate if their output will conform to the Epub3 standards.

To self-publish a book, you need a packager. Packagers and publishers are not the same thing.

With a publisher, you submit a manuscript and the publisher, after reading the content, either rejects it or accepts it. If accepted, the publisher will perform all the tasks and absorb all the expense of producing the finished book.

A packager takes your manuscript file and the cover file and puts them together to produce the book. Packagers are not concerned with the content of the manuscript and will not reject any manuscript unless it violates their submission guidelines. Some packagers will offer assistance with covers and other aspects of publishing, but these services always come with a price.

Kindle is a packager, so is IngramSpark and Smashwords Packagers are discussed in more depth in Chapter 4.

The process of self-publishing a quality book package may seem daunting at first blush, but thousands of other authors have pulled it off. So why can't you? If you were capable enough to write a book, you're capable enough to self-publish your book.

Don't give up!

Epub3 Standard

The Epub3 standard has been developed by a global organization that sets the rules for ebooks. The standard defines how ebooks can embed graphics, audio clips and video tracks, and it has very strict formatting rules. Many book sellers such as Barnes & Noble and iBooks will not accept an ebook that doesn't conform to the Epub3 standards.

This standard wasn't put in place with authors in mind. Rather its purpose is make reading an ebook on a tablet or e-reader pleasurable. That means authors have to ensure their ebook manuscripts are compliant with the standard.

Epub3 formatting is covered in Chapter 6

Book Marketing

To an author who is embarking on her first self-publishing project, book marketing is probably an area that is far from her mind. However, book marketing isn't something you address after you finish publishing the book. Marketing should start long in advance of the book's launch date.

Once this horrible thought has settled into your mind, you can begin to appreciate this situation. Yes, it makes sense to tell people about the book before it can be bought. Yes, it makes sense to get potential readers interested in the book as early as possible.

Here is another tidbit: thousands of books will be published the day your book is published. No one will know about your book and no one will care about it. The whole point of book marketing is to tell people (i.e. readers) about your book and to make them care enough to buy a copy.

In other words, you will have to venture into the marsh land known as marketing, and you need to avoid the alligators and poisonous snakes. And you will have to jump in and start paddling while you're still working at getting the book ready to be published.

But don't panic. This book will guide you through the marsh land and get you safely to the other side with your sanity intact.

Budgeting

Before we get too far into the plan let's talk money. Your money. Publishing and marketing a book cost money. The publishing aspect has some mandatory expenses. There are some publishing tasks that will be free if you have the technical expertise (and the time) to do them yourself.

Many marketing tasks are free while others will come with a price. A few marketing tasks will cost a bundle of money. That's why you need to establish a budget: to see which tasks you can afford and which ones to ignore.

So why do we work on a budget in the beginning of the project? It's possible you'll need time to gather the funds necessary to support your publishing and marketing activities. The earlier you understand the costs of the project, the less likely you are to experience unpleasant surprises later on.

Publishing Budget

Your publishing budget has two mandatory items and a number of other items that may or may not require funding. The two mandatory items are a book cover and professional editing.

Book covers are important because in many cases the first contact a buyer has with your book is seeing the cover on some website like Amazon. A dull cover will not grab that buyer's attention. A unique cover will perhaps get the buyer to look more closely at your book. Surveys indicate a substantial number of buyers investigate a book because of the cover. My advice is this: Don't skimp on the cover. Spend as much as you can afford to get a unique cover for your book. I advise you to ignore the inexpensive, generic covers that are available on the web. A generic cover tells a potential reader the content is also generic. An example of generic covers is the pre-made ones available on many websites. There is more on covers in Chapter 3.

Editing will be the largest expense in the publishing project. A good editor can change your content from amateurish-looking writing to a more polished manuscript. Nothing tells a reader the author is an amateur faster than a lot of typos and incorrect words. As examples, consider *to, too* and *two*. Or *fore* and *four*. Do not count on spellcheck to save the day and don't ask a friend to edit the book unless that friend is also a professional editor.

Other expenses such as formatting and book design may not occur if you have the technical expertise to do it yourself or have a software program to help out.

An ISBN may be required. If so it can cost a chunk of money in the United States. ISBN stands for International Standard Book Number. Oftentimes, however, it is possible to get a free ISBN. More about ISBNs in Chapter 6.

Here is a list of budget *estimates* for the publishing end of your project:

<u>Mandatory charges</u>:
- Ebook cover: $50+
- Print cover: $150+
- Editing: $350 to over $1,000 depending on a range of factors

<u>Possible charges</u>
- Packager setup fees: $25-$100
- Distribution fees: $25-$75
- Book design: $50+
- Formatting: $50+
- ISBN: $0 to $125
- Packager conversion services: $150+

Packager and distribution fees are used by some packagers. Most packagers do not charge for these services. Packagers are discussed in Chapter 6.

If you plan on publishing an ebook and a print book, the covers will cost less than the sum of the two covers shown above. This is because the ebook cover is also the front of the print book cover.

If you plan an ebook and a print book, you'll need two ISBNs.

Marketing Budget

The marketing budget is harder to put together than the publishing budget. This is because a number of the marketing items are nebulous and variable. Many of them can be considered optional. There are also a myriad of potential marketing activities you can deploy and not all of them cost money.

Here is a list of marketing activities that cost money. You can use these to help put together an estimate.

- Website development: $200 + unless you can do it yourself, then $0. (See Chapter 4)
- Website hosting and URL: $50 per year. (See Chapter 4)
- Website security: $100/year (if you start your own web site) (See Chapter 4)
- Book review services: $25 to $100 each (See Chapter 8)
- Blog tour: $200-$1000+ depending upon the company used and the length of the tour (See Chapter 4)
- Trailers (similar to movie trailers): $50 to several hundred dollars depending upon length and quality unless you can do it yourself, then $0) (See Chapter 6)
- Book giveaways: $25-100 (See Chapter 8)
- Social media ads: $25-$100 depending upon the site and the length of the ad. (See Chapter 8)
- Publicist: $4000 + (See Chapter 8)

Most of these bullet items are explained in some depth later on, but for now, let's say a few words about them.

You'll need a website of some sort. This isn't optional. If your decision is to create your own website, (rather than use a shared one) then you must consider a security service because the internet swarms with trolls who will try to hijack your site.

At a minimum, I recommend you allocate at least $200 or $300 to promote your book. These funds should be used on a website, book giveaways, book reviews and social media ads. If you have money left after funding the minimum, use it on a trailer, a blog tour or a publicist. Alternatively, you can decide to spend that extra money on more giveaways, review or ads.

Whatever you do, do NOT take out a second mortgage to pay for the book marketing.

What's Next?

Now that you've established your budgets and understand some basic concepts, you can move on to the first publishing and marketing tasks. There are a number of initial tasks for the publishing part of the project and one vital task for the marketing piece. This task is to develop a strategic marketing plan and it will require some time and research to complete it, but it's free.

Chapter 2: 6 Months Before Launch

Overview

This part of the project deals with tasks that should be worked on and completed six months before the launch date. Beginning your first self-publishing project is actually an exciting time. You're finally finished writing and revising your book and you are about to embark on a new venture.

As you start your self-publishing project, you will come across tasks that are outside your experiences as an author. This is to be expected since the only commonality between writing a book, self-publishing the book and marketing the book is that all these activities involve the same book and the same person.

Publishing is the process of getting your book into a form that the reading public can read and buy.

The goal of self-publishing is to produce a quality book package to hold your quality content. To achieve this, you have to ensure the self-publishing tasks are completed as perfectly as possible. This will involve time and money. And it just isn't your time we're talking about. Others are involved in the process and their time has to be factored into the project.

These others involved include beta readers, cover artists and editors. These people may be sympathetic to your launch date but they have their own problems and workloads.

One task you'll have to work on is formatting the ebook manuscript. The formatting has to be done in accordance with the Epub3 standard and that can be a difficult and tedious process. It may also require outside help. Hiring such an expert represents another possible interval that has to be accounted for.

The process of self-publishing a quality book bundle may seem daunting at first blush, but thousands of other authors have pulled it off. So why can't you? If you were capable enough to write a book, I think you're capable enough to self-publish your book.

Initial book marketing tasks consist of developing material that will be used later on when the marketing activities intensify. Getting it done early lightens the work load later on.

The publish tasks covered in this chapter include:
- Establish the launch date
- Finish the manuscript
- Recruit beta readers

Under marketing, the task is:
- Develop a strategic plan

Publishing Tasks

Establish the Launch Date

Self-publishing means you are the publisher in addition to being the author.

Since you are the publisher, you decide the launch date at which time the world will be able to purchase a copy of your book. Now is a good time to choose that date. It will have to be far enough away to enable you to complete all the tasks in the publishing and marketing project. This means you have to resist the urge to make the launch date next week! Releasing a book that doesn't yet have a quality book package is self-defeating. It will turn off potential buyers.

So now your job (as the publisher) is to select the launch date. The most important factor to consider is whether or not you will have time to complete all the work involved. Life frequently interferes with this work so the date at this point is an educated guess. But since you are the publisher, you can move the launch date out if you are having trouble making it. You can also move it closer if situation warrants that. If you can link your book to a popular holiday, that will be great boost. For instance, if your book's setting is around Christmas time, a December launch is appropriate. But that means you have to start on the project in May in order to make the December launch date.

For now, decide on what the tentative launch date will be.

Finish the Manuscript

This may strike you as a silly task. Of course your manuscript is finished. Or is it?

If your manuscript is a first draft, it is NOT finished. As Pulitzer winning novelist Ernest Hemingway put it, "The first draft of anything is a piece of shit." Publishing a first draft runs counter to the premise of producing and publishing a quality book package.

How many drafts does it take to finish the manuscript? That is an unanswerable question. In my own case, no one sees my work until I've written the third draft at least. After that beta readers get a chance to poke holes in it.

One test for completeness is to go through it one more time. If you don't see any mistakes and you don't get an urge to rewrite a paragraph or a scene, it's as good as you can make it. However, just because you don't see any mistakes does not mean beta readers and a professional editor won't find problems. More about those issues later.

For some writers, letting go is a traumatic event; they want to continue to revise and revise some more. To these writers, the book never seems 'done.' When writers continue to revise a book, they'll eventually reach a point where their efforts are detrimental to the work: they are actually dis-improving the book.

Usually, my books are 'done' by the fourth or fifth draft: and that includes the beta reader revisions. After that, it's time for an editor to take a look at it. In one case, my book went through eight revisions before sending it to an editor.

To summarize, the author has to take a leap of faith and decide at some point the book is 'done' and it's time to move on.

Once you decide the manuscript is finished, it's time to find beta readers.

Recruit Beta Readers

One milestone in writing a book is reaching a point where you can hire a content editor to examine it. However, content editors are expensive, perhaps prohibitively so.

An alternative to hiring a content editor is to recruit other writers and ask them to critique your work. Critiquers are also called beta readers by some folks, including me.

One mistake inexperienced writers often make is to ask family members to comment on the story. Besides the potential for embarrassing the family members, these readers can't offer any advice on how to improve the book.

While some readers may have a good sense on what works for them, they don't have the background to tell an author 'why' it worked or didn't work. The reader may not like a character or get turned off by the plot, but statements like that are too vague to be of much use to the author. The author needs to hear why the character is not likable (too many bad habits perhaps). As for the plot, there are many factors that can make it go awry. These include: illogical developments, twists that aren't properly developed and explained, irrational actions by the characters, reactions not properly foreshadowed and many more. If the author gets feedback from other writers or trusted fans on these factors, the author can take steps to fix the problems.

In the case of a non-fiction book, the author can look to subject matter experts for critical comments.

Beta readers will often agree to work on your story in return for you taking a look at their book. Thus, it's a *quid pro quid* arrangement. It is best to have a team of beta readers. Six is a good number of readers to have. They will give you a range of comments and opinions to look at. More is good, but you may have to settle for less.

The comments from the beta readers will identify problems that must be addressed. If they do their job correctly, they will likely tear your book apart and that can be a painful process for the inexperienced author who probably thinks the work is already damn-near perfect.

Beta reader comments also present the author with a decision that has to be made: are the comments valid or not? It is not unusual to come across an occasional comment that will not improve the book and can be safely ignored. Other comments may actually dis-improve it if implemented.

It is the author's responsibility to weigh the comments with an open mind and choose the ones that will make the manuscript stronger and better. Keep in mind that readers will bring their own set of prejudices and perspectives to your work. If the group as a whole makes the same comment, you should take it seriously. If a comment comes from only a single reader, you'll have to decide if it's relevant or not.

Oftentimes, this selection process will result in major revisions that must be incorporated into the book before the publishing process can move forward. You certainly don't want to send the unrevised manuscript to an editor, and you certainly don't want to spend time formatting a version that will have dramatic changes in it later on

This is why it is necessary to recruit and use beta readers as early as possible. I recruit my beta readers and use their comments to revise the manuscript before I start the publication tasks.

Ask the beta readers to return their comments within a month, a reasonable request unless they are in the middle of their own publishing process.

For a novel, I send my beta readers a list of questions I'd like them to answer after they finish reading the manuscript. The questionnaire is listed here:

Please answer as many questions as you feel are relevant. There is no need to answer ALL of the questions (unless you want to)

1: Did the story hold your interest from the very beginning? If not, why not?

2: Did you get oriented fairly quickly at the beginning as to whose story it is, and where and when it's taking place? If not, why not?

3: Could you relate to the main character? Did you feel her/his pain or excitement?

4: Did the setting interest you and did the descriptions seem vivid and real to you?

5: Was there a point at which you felt the story lagged or you became less than excited about finding out what was going to happen next? Where, exactly?

6: Were there any parts that confused you? Or even frustrated or annoyed you? Which parts, and why?

7: Did you notice any discrepancies or inconsistencies in time sequences, places, character details, or other details?

8: Were the characters believable? Are there any characters you think could be made more interesting or more likable?

9: Did you get confused about who's who in the characters? Were there too many characters to keep track of? Too few? Are any of the names of characters too similar?

10: Did the dialogue keep your interest and sound natural to you? If not, whose dialogue did you think sounded artificial or not like that person would speak?

11: Did you feel there was too much description or exposition? Not enough? Maybe too much dialogue in parts?

12: Was there enough conflict, tension, and intrigue to keep your interest?

13: Was the ending satisfying? Believable?

14: Did you notice any obvious repeating grammatical, spelling, punctuation or capitalization errors? Examples?

15: Did you think the writing style suits the genre? If not, why not?

16: Did I introduce too many characters in the first scene?

This list is based on https://writingcooperative.com/15-questions-to-send-beta-first-readers-please-steal-3ff9fa198b5

Marketing Tasks

Develop a Strategic Marketing Plan

To begin, you will have to make a decision on whether or not you will actively market your book or ignore all marketing concerns. The idea of marketing your book may be disheartening, but it's what happens when you publish a book. Thousands of other authors have faced this same decision and survived it and so can you.

A major component of the marketing decision concerns why you wrote the book. If your purpose is to check off an item on your bucket list, then marketing may not be for you. If your purpose was to give the book as a gift to your family and a few friends, then marketing may not be one of your concerns. In these cases, you can probably skip the marketing and concentrate on the publishing tasks. If, on the other hand, your objective in writing the book was to sell copies and gain a measure of name recognition, then marketing is something you have to embrace. Read on.

My objective in writing this book is to provide a resource for new authors interested in self-publishing their book. So, yes, I want to sell books and therefore, I accept that I have to market the book, even though writing another novel would be more fun.

Marketing for the unwary is fraught with financial peril. It is quite easy to unwittingly spend money on "services" that are no value to you or your readers. This happens most frequently to authors who don't have a marketing plan for their book. In these cases, desperate to get sales, they dump money into marketing schemes or scams that will have no impact on book sales. Having a strategic marketing plan will help protect you from these types of money wasters.

Let's talk about another perplexing issue: Does book marketing work?

The short answer is: yes, it does. One of the objectives of your marketing efforts will be to tell potential buyers about your book. Without marketing, these people would never have heard about it and hence would never have bought the book. Think about how many ads you see on TV and the web introducing a new product. The purpose of the ads is to tell people that this new product exists and they should buy it. It's the same with your book. You have to tell people it exists. In effect, every book you sell is the result of the marketing tactics you deployed, even if the marketing tactic was simply telling a guy at a coffee shop about your book.

One of the frustrating aspects of marketing is that you never know which tactic resulted in a book sale. Was the sale triggered by a blog post? By a tweet? By watching the trailer? You'll never know. It's quite possible the sale was triggered by all three tactics over a period of time. Studies have shown that sales are often the result of repeated exposure to a product's ads. There are many websites devoted to tracking visits, clicks, downloads and other social media measurements, but they won't tell you *who* bought the book. Packagers such as Amazon and the others will not tell you who bought the book even though they know who it was.

Your first marketing task is to develop a strategic marketing plan to guide the rest of your efforts. The strategic plan consists of defining your customers and the market where your book will compete against many other books.

The initial thing you need to know about marketing a book is that it can't be a half-hearted effort involving an occasional email or blog post, stuff you send out when you don't have anything better to do. You have to dedicate a chunk of time, effort and, yes, money, to market the book. Why do you need the completed marketing plan so early? Because you need to start the marketing efforts long before the book is published.

I suggest you copy these bullet items and paste them into a word processor and then write your answers. That way, you'll have a permanent file you can use to refresh your memory. It will also be useful when you write a second book. Or you can use the spreadsheet I developed to record your answers and simplify the work you have to do. It has sample answers to make your life a bit simpler. To get a copy, send me an email hanque (at) gmail (dot) com. It's available in .xls format.

Some of the answers to the questions require information contained in later chapters. As a consequence, you may not be able to complete the strategic plan until after you finish reading this book. That's okay as long as the plan is fully developed before you start the marketing efforts because the strategic plan is your marketing roadmap and it will define which marketing tactics you deploy.

Marketing Plan: Product, Customers and Competitors:
- Describe the book.
- What's different about the book?
- What benefit does the customer get from buying your book?
- Why would a customer buy your book instead of a competitor's book?
- Who are your competitors?
- What benefits do they offer?
- How is your book better than the competitor's book?
- Who are your target customers?
- What sales channels will you use to sell your book?
- What marketing channels will you use to reach your targeted customers?
- What will your book be priced at?
- How does your price compare to the competitor's price?

Marketing Plan: Objectives and Budgets:
- What are the financial objectives for this plan?
- How will you measure these financial results?
- What are the secondary objectives for this plan?
- How will you measure the results?
- What is your marketing budget for year 1?
- What is your marketing budget for year 2?

What's different about the book?

This question and the two that follow are critically important questions. In Chapter 5, you'll use the answers to develop an important marketing message called the book blurb. For now, come up with answers to the questions.

Who are your target customers?

Let's talk in more detail about the identification of customers. The first step in the development of a marketing plan is to identify who the customers are and what problem your book will solve for those customers.

Once you stop groaning, we will proceed.

If you have written a non-fiction book, you must have had a set of potential readers in mind. For instance, if you have written a book about fixing household plumbing, your potential readers are people who live in homes with leaky faucets or pipes. Or people who suspect they will have leak problems someday. Your customers are the plumbing-needy and your book will solve the customers' needs for plumbing advice.

If you wrote a book about how to do surgery at home on the kitchen table, your target readership is a bit more limited. Possibly it'll be folks who don't have health insurance although I'm not sure this book will solve the customer's problem. It may actually worsen their problem.

If you wrote a children's picture book, you may think the kids are the customers; they're not. Kids don't have money or credit cards. Kids don't browse bookstores or websites. Your customers are the parents and grandparents. Other family members and close friends are also customers.

If your book is a fictional tale, you have to position it depending upon the potential audience. Romance readers are quite different from mystery fans and so are sci-fi aficionados. In either case, your book will entertain the reader which is a way of solving a problem for the customer. It gives them a break from reality.

Once you identify your readership, the rest of the marketing plan will be aimed at that group of people, not the general population.

What sales channels will you use to sell your book?

This question refers to the packagers you will use. Packagers are covered in Chapter 4

What marketing channels will you use to reach your targeted customers?

Marketing channels refer primarily to social media sites you will use to reach the customers. Chapter 3 has details on this issue.

Marketing Plan Objectives

Another early step in market plan development is to establish a set of financial objectives. A business needs to set goals for itself and if you haven't realized it yet, let me point out that once you publish a book, you own a business and the purpose of this business is to market and sell your book. There is more on author business issues in Chapter 9.

The reality facing a first-time self-published author is that you won't sell many books in the near term even though, over time, you may indeed sell truckloads of books. For this reason, you should establish goals that recognize this reality and keep your initial goals modest.

While a business may have non-financial goals, they are secondary to the financial goals. Such goals can be: get interviewed on a local radio or TV show; have a book signing in a book store.

An important consideration is that the objectives must be measurable. Another consideration is that they must be reasonable and achievable. Setting goals that can't be reached is simply an exercise in futility. However, the goals must be hard enough to reach that they will force you to turn off the TV and work on meeting the goals.

Don't make the mistake I made when I self-published my first book. I decided to delay implementing the marketing plans until I sold enough books to pay for the marketing costs. Bummer! I didn't sell any books. The lesson leaned is that the marketing comes first and book sales follow. In other words, you have to spend time and money in order to make money.

Save your strategic plan. When you write a second book, you can reuse it and only have to change the budget information unless your next book is a different genre from the first book. If, for instance, your first book was a sci-fi novel and your second is a murder mystery, you need to redefine your customers. If your second book is non-fiction, you'll have to re-do most of the strategic plan.

Chapter 3: 5 Months Before Launch

Overview

At the five month milestone, it's time to undertake a few preliminary tasks that will be necessary to get the book published.

For the marketing phase, it's time to establish a presence on the web.

Social media is an essential part of your marketing plan and your branding. However, be warned. Social media is a major time suck and many sites are next to worthless when it comes to marketing and selling your book. Nevertheless, you must persist. Later in this chapter, I'll talk about a few social media sites you should start to use if you aren't already on them.

There is a reason for you to set up these accounts so far in advance of the launch date. It gives you time to connect with people and grow the number of contacts you have on each platform. This will increase the number of people you can tell about the book. After all, the primary function of the social media sites is to spread the word about you and your book, so the more people you can tell, the better.

If you prowl around the web, you'll find many author and writer sites that sound attractive. A large number of them are sites where authors try to get other authors to buy their books. Almost every post or notice is a variation of 'Buy my book, please.' I consider these sites as more than useless because they won't help you with marketing the book and they have the potential to waste gobs of time.

In this chapter we'll cover these publishing tasks:
- Revise the manuscript

- Get a book cover

The marketing tasks discussed are:

- Create a Goodreads account
- Create a Facebook account
- Join LinkedIn
- Establish a Twitter account
- Explore other social media sites

Publishing Tasks

Revise the Manuscript

If your beta readers returned their comments within a month, now is the time to revise your manuscript to include their recommendations. This can take some time to accomplish, but you can still revise it and stay on track with the publication plan.

If you worked with a number of beta readers and you now have a pile of comments to work through, this can be a confusing process. The process is made more difficult because some of the comments are probably contradictory.

Here is how I go about working my way through such a pile of beta reader material.

A first step in making the revisions is to determine whether each comment is relevant or should be ignored. Next, give each beta reader a code (such as their initials), go through the unrevised manuscript and indicate where each beta reader made a comment. Granted, this may take several passes, but in the end, the unrevised manuscript will show where you have to make the changes. You may prefer to do this chapter by chapter rather than doing the entire manuscript. Once you're finished marking up the manuscript, you're ready to start revising it.

Get a Book Cover

A quality book cover is an important element in getting your book noticed. Studies have shown that many readers are initially attracted to a book by the cover. Consequently, a shoddy cover won't attract potential readers.

My advice is to hire a competent cover artist to create a unique cover for your book. If you already know such an artist, great. In this case, you may be able to get a unique cover at an attractive price. If you don't know such an artist or if you can't afford a hefty expense, the question comes down to this: How do you find someone who can produce the cover for your book? The usual way to find such an artist is to use the internet.

A web search can produce a slew of names for artists willing to work on your book. I don't recommend contacting any of these names. Why? There is a possibility that some of the names aren't legitimate artists but are rather scammers hoping to get contacted to make some money. Other names will be mediocre artists who will oversell their ability.

In your web searches, you'll find a number of artists who have produced a number of pre-made ebook covers you can buy at an inexpensive price. Once you pay for it, the artist will add your title and name to the cover and send it to you. While this may sound like an ideal solution, it comes with a few drawbacks. First, the covers are generic and won't match your story very well. Second, a generic cover tells the potential buyer the content will also be generic. Third, the artist retains the copyright to the cover blank and can sell it again to another author. So there is a strong possibility you will see 'your' cover on someone else's book.

I recommend you use a third approach to find your cover artist: ask on LinkedIn and Goodreads author or writing groups for recommendations. (More about these websites later in this chapter). The names you receive will be for cover artists who have previously worked with the recommender. Once you get some names, send an email describing your project and any ideas about what you'd like to see on the cover. With my cover artist, I describe the cover in a paragraph or two and then let him go crazy turning my words into a picture. We work well this way and he frequently captures my ideas on the first pass.

If you look at the back cover on a print book, you'll see that it is filled with text. Would you like to hazard a guess who writes that text? That's right, you do. The back text has to be completed before the cover artist can finish the cover file. This back cover is an ideal place to put a book blurb, which is a short marketing pitch to grab the interest of people who pick up your book and browse the covers. Book blurbs will be discussed in Chapter 5.

Print covers are more complicated than ebook covers. With ebooks, you only need a graphic for the front cover. Print book covers, on the other hand, have three parts: the front cover (same as the ebook cover), a back cover and a spine between the two. In addition, print books come in a number of sizes and the size must be determined before you can get cover. There is more on print book sizes in Chapter 6 under Complete the Book Design.

The spine is the tricky part. The width has to be calculated, and that width depends upon how many pages are in the book and the thickness of the paper used. Packagers have a standard page thickness which will be shown somewhere on their website, and you can use that number to calculate the spine thickness by using a spine calculator. One such calculator can be found at: https://www.bookmobile.com/book-spine-width-calculator/. Book packagers like Kindle and IngramSpark have a calculator that allows you to come up with the correct figure. Once you get the thickness number, save it because your cover artist needs it to produce the cover.

The final print cover will be in pdf format and ready to upload to your packager, who will merge it with your text file. It looks a bit weird when you see one for the first time. On the left side of the file is the back cover. In the middle is the spine, and the front cover is on the right side of the graphic. On the back cover, notice the unused space at the lower right corner next to the spine. This is where the bar code and the ISBN go. The packager will add this when the book is printed. ISBN stands for International Standard Book Number. More about ISBN's in Chapter 6.

This is the way I work with my cover artist. I tell him what I want on the front cover (which is also the ebook cover), and he works up a sketch and sends it to me for comments. When we agree on what the cover will look like, he sends me a picture file of the front cover. I use this to put on websites and to begin my marketing efforts. Later on, if I plan a print book as well as an ebook, I tell him the book size, the spine width and the back cover text. From this he produces the complete print cover file.

I pay him half of the agreed upon price when the front (ebook) cover is completed. I pay the second half when the entire cover is finished and delivered to me. I get the ebook cover as early as possible so I can begin marketing the book. There may be a gap of several months between the time I get the front cover and the time I get the finished cover file. That's why I pay the cover artist in two bites. He has to eat, too.

All my covers are made by a guy on the West Coast named Gary Tenuta. You can contact him at gvtgrafix@aol.com. Here is a link to his website where you can review his portfolio: http://bookcoversandvideos.webs.com/

A completed print book cover file is shown below.

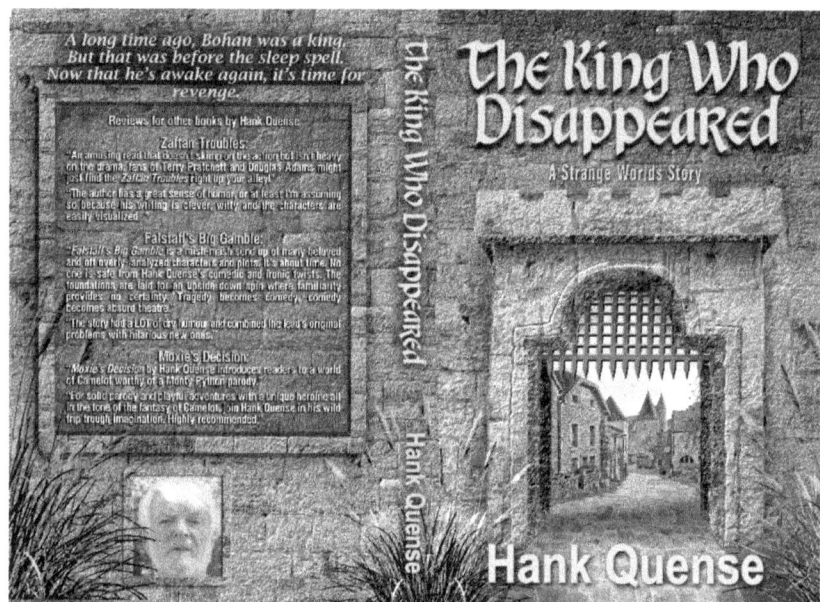

The book size for this cover is 5.5 inches by 8.5 inches. Book size is a matter of preference and there are a lot of sizes to choose from.

MarketingTasks

Create a Goodreads Account

Goodreads is a place for readers and authors to interact. You can find it by using this link: https://www.goodreads.com.

The great thing about the readers on this site is that they write book reviews. Hold that thought; we'll discuss it further in a bit. Once you have your account set up, start using it by joining the author program. This will enable you to establish an author page with a bio, book listings and other information. Later, you can run book giveaways, join reader and writer groups, and engage in discussions. You'll find the author program here: https://www.goodreads.com/author/program

After you get the book cover and develop the blurb and short synopsis for your soon-to-be released book, add them to Goodreads and list the expected publication date. If your book sounds interesting (i.e. you have added compelling material), other members will start to list the book as 'want to read.' Send a 'friend request' to those members because your Goodreads friends will get a message when you post a review, run a book sale or schedule an event.

Goodreads has numerous groups covering just about every conceivable aspect of reading and publishing books. Join a few of these groups and participate in the threads. You can schedule events such as a book launch and send a message to your friends about the event.

Goodreads is one of the better social media sites.

Another site for readers and authors is Librarything, but it isn't as robust as Goodreads. You can find it here: https://www.librarything.com

Create a FaceBook Account

You may already have a Facebook account; it seems most people do. If so, what you have is called a personal account. If you don't have one, go to https://www.facebook.com and start a personal account.

Facebook also has an option called 'Pages' and you want one, but you can't start it until you also have a personal account. Pages can be started for businesses, music groups, community groups and even authors. You can start one for your book or, better yet, start it for yourself as an author. That way you can add information about your second book without starting another page.

Once you start the page, add your book cover, your differentiation statement and new reviews as you get them. On your page you'll have the ability to post content similar to the way a blog operates. Use this feature to post new reviews and other content.

On your personal account, ask friends to like the page. This will increase the number of potential buyers who see the page.

Establish a Twitter Account

Twitter is quite different from the previous social media sites discussed. You can find Twitter here: https://twitter.com

On Twitter, you post short messages that are 280 characters or less. There are a lot of authors and writers on Twitter, and you should spend time finding ones that write in your genre and connect with them.

You can post tweets (as they're called) on just about any possible topic, and as you add people to follow you'll start to see some strange stuff in your feed. You'll also see messages that are relevant to your book and writing career. You can reply to these and that can be the start of a conversation on the topic. It will take some time for you to adjust to Twitter and to get comfortable with it.

When you follow someone on Twitter, you'll see their tweets. When someone follows you, they will see your tweets. As you follow more people, you'll notice their tweets don't stay on the screen very long. As more tweets are received, the ones you're looking at will get pushed lower on the screen.

Studies have shown that different audiences look at Twitter at different times of the day. So, if you have an important message you want to get out, post it several times during the day. Make each message slightly different from the preceding ones or Twitter will display a message that you already sent the message out.

An important part of Twitter is hashtags. These are words or phrases preceded by a # (#amwriting is a popular hashtag). Hashtags are Twitter talk for keywords. You can add one or two hashtags (or more) to your tweet so people interested in that hashtag can find it. If you click on a hashtag in a tweet, you'll see a list of current tweets on that subject.

Some of the hashtags I use are:

#fantasy

#scifi

#humor

#satire

#amwriting

#publishing

#selfpublishing

There are many, many more hashtags you can employ. As you use Twitter, you'll come across more or them and become comfortable using them.

Join LinkedIn

LinkedIn is a site for professionals from all types of businesses including the writing and publishing industries. It's quite different from Facebook. You'll find it at this web location: https://www.linkedin.com

After you sign up, browse the site to gain an understanding, then search for writing and publishing groups. There are a lot of them, so be selective. Don't join them all or you'll be overwhelmed with emails. The value of these groups is that you can ask questions and get useful information from the other group members. Most importantly, you can ask for names of editors or cover artists. The names you get will be ones who have been used by the other LinkedIn members and aren't likely to be scam artists.

You can also ask questions on almost any aspect of writing and publishing and you'll get responses. If, as you browse the web, you come across an 'interesting' marketing offer, ask in the groups if anyone has experience or has interacted with the offerer. The responses may clarify if the offer is legitimate or not.

When you ask questions about writing, publishing or marketing, the responses will contradict each other oftentimes. That reflects the wealth of experiences of the other members and that's what makes life interesting.

Over time, your LinkedIn contact list will expand and the site will become more valuable to you. Just lurking and reading the questions and responses will teach you a lot and will give you ideas and leads.

LinkedIn uses hashtags similar to Twitter.

Explore Other Social Media Sites

There are many other websites you can join such as Pinterest, Instagram and others that spring up ever day. Join them or not as you want. You may find these sites are more for personal use than marketing related.

The more sites you join, the more time you will spend on them. Remember the statement in the overview to this chapter? "Social media is a major time suck."

Perhaps there is a better way to use your time rather than joining too many social media sites, but that is a personal choice.

Chapter 4: 4 Months Before Launch

Overview

With four months to go, there are more tasks to be worked on in both the publishing and the marketing categories.

To prepare for the big day, it's time to look at packagers and to hire an editor. Both of these tasks will require research on your part. For the marketing effort, you have to create a webpage.

The publishing tasks are:
- Select packagers
- Using packager conversion services
- Getting paid
- Print on demand
- Hire an editor

The marketing chores:
- Create a web site

Publishing Tasks

Packagers

If you are self-publishing, you need a packager. Packagers and publishers are not the same things. If a publisher bought your manuscript you don't need a packager because the publisher will do everything a packager would do. If you plan to self-publish both an ebook and a print book, you may need two packagers.

What does a packager do? It performs several vital functions. Initially, you upload the manuscript and the cover file to the packager, who puts the files together to produce the ebook or print book. Once the book is released, the packager distributes the book to various sellers. Whenever one of the sellers records a sale, the packager receives the sales revenue, accumulates it and sends you a royalty check, usually once a month.

Both the seller and the packager keep part of the sales revenue and you get the rest.

There are a number of packagers available, and the numbers keep changing as some pop up while others disappear. A web search will provide lists of packagers to choose from. Don't sign up with the first ones you come across since not all the packagers are reputable and some may actually be vanity press outfits masquerading as a legitimate packager. The issue with vanity presses is that they aren't interested in your book. They are only interested in how much money they can siphon out of your wallet.

A vanity press, and there are many of them, is a publisher/packager who is only interested in how thick your wallet is. They'll publish anything, no matter how bad it is, as long as the author can pay the multi-thousand dollar fees. Besides the publishing fees, they will also suck the author into buying expensive marketing programs. Another tactic widely used by vanity press publishers is to insist contractually that the author purchase hundreds of print books at inflated prices. I recommend you avoid all vanity presses. Actually, the vanity presses are easy to spot: they advertise. If you visit a website and see an ad for a publishing company, it most certainly is a vanity press.

For my ebooks, I use two packagers: Smashwords and Kindle. Why two? I do that in order to increase the number of markets that sell my books.

Kindle distributes ebooks only within the Amazon universe. At the moment, that universe includes 13 world-wide markets in Europe, Central and South America, Asia and Australia.

Smashwords distributes ebooks to non-Amazon sites such as Barnes & Noble, iBooks, Kobo and a number of other sites.

For print books, I use two other packagers: IngramSpark and Createspace, now Kindle. The major distinction between these two is that IngramSpark distributes print books to Ingram and Baker & Taylor. Ingram is used by many bookstores and Baker & Taylor deals mostly with libraries. Kindle is a Amazon company and distributes to other Amazon sites such as the UK, Germany and Japan. (Before you ask, when Kindle distributes to foreign markets such as Japan, they do not translate your book into Japanese. It's only available in English.)

An important difference between IngramSpark and Kindle is this. With IngramSpark you have a chance of getting your book carried by bookstores. With Kindle, you have no chance of getting the book into bookstores. Why? Because Kindle won't allow the bookstores to discount as deeply as they are accustomed to and because Kindle won't allow bookstores to return books. These two factors result in bookstores' refusal to handle Kindle print books.

When considering a packager, study the submission guidelines. If you don't adhere to the submission guidelines exactly, your submission will be rejected.

Just because I list my packagers here doesn't mean you shouldn't do your own research. Consider my packagers as your starting point.

In addition, make sure you read *ALL* the fine print on the website. In the website's fine print, you may find onerous conditions, and it's devastating to find out about those conditions after you sign a contract or agree to the

Terms and Conditions statement. One possible onerous condition for print book packagers is that you agree to buy a large number of print books at an outrageous price. I've seen this condition on a number of print book publishers sites and it's possible some print packagers now use it, also.

Here is a list of questions to ask or search for answers when considering a packager.

- What distributors do they use, if any? Barnes & Noble? Kobo? iBooks?
- Are the distributors optional? If so, how are they activated?
- Is there a fee associated with the distribution process? If so, how much?
- Does the packager provide any marketing efforts on your behalf? If yes, what are these efforts?
- Does the packager charge for marketing assistance? And how much?
- What is the revenue split from the packager sales?
- What is the revenue split from distributor sales?
- How frequently does the packager disburse sales revenue? Monthly? Quarterly?
- Is there a minimum value before the packager will disburse sales revenue?
- Where will you find sales reports? Online? In an email?
- Will the packager provide an ISBN for your book? Is it free? If not free, how much do they charge for the ISBN?

The distributor question is important because the answer reveals where buyers can find your book on the internet besides the packager's web site. Typical distributors are Kindle, iStore and Barnes & Noble. There are other smaller distributors in addition to the ones listed above.. All of these distributor sites will have a page displaying your book cover, your book blurb and perhaps an author bio. If a visitor to one if these sites clicks on the buy-button, money is collected and a copy of your book is downloaded to the buyer's computer or mobile device. The site keeps a piece of the sales revenue and forwards the remainder to your packager.

By the way, the packager does *not* have exclusive rights to your book. You can sell copies on your own or even give away copies if you choose. Just because you used Kindle for your ebook doesn't mean you can't also use Smashwords or any other packager.

Be aware that Kindle has an exclusive feature called Kindle Select. It gives Kindle the exclusive rights to your book for three months. In this case you *cannot* also use Smashwords. This exclusive feature also automatically renews unless you manually find and unselect the feature.

At this point if you know which packagers you will use, you can start accounts with them.

Using packager conversion services

In recent developments, print packagers now offer to convert your print book into an ebook and ebook packagers offer to convert your ebook into a print book.

IngramSpark will convert your print book into an Epub3 compliant ebook, but they will charge you for the service. Currently, the charge is $0.60 per print page. So if your print book has 300 pages the conversion service will cost you $180. You will also have to provide a new, unused ISBN.

Kindle also has conversion services. They will convert a print book to an ebook and an ebook to a print book. Of course, to convert an ebook, you'll have to have a print book cover. In converting a print book to an ebook, Kindle will not create an Epub3 compliant ebook. Kindle will create a .mobi edition which is only used within the Amazon universe. In other words, your converted ebook will not be compatible with the submission guidelines of other packagers like Smashwords, Barnes & Noble, iBooks and others.

Other packagers most likely offer conversion services as do a number of websites. There is a growth in the number companies who will convert your manuscript into an ebook, either epub or mobi and/or a print book. These companies charge for these services and most are based on a price per manuscript page. Use the search function on your browser to find them.

I don't use any conversion services since I prepare both a print book manuscript and an ebook manuscript.

If you decide to use these conversion services, make sure your budget can afford it.

Getting Paid

This is an important consideration. After all, you never know when you may sell some books and actually earn royalties. You have to be prepared for that eventuality. There are a number of ways that you can receive money from your book sales.

One way to receive money is directly from people who buy your book at events, appearances and lectures. You give them a book, preferably signed, and they hand you cash, a check or a credit/debit card if you have the capability to handle it. This is the simplest and most lucrative method of selling a book since you don't have to split the revenue with a distributor or packager. However, reality says your appearances will most likely be geographically limited and so will these types of sales.

A word about sales taxes would be appropriate at this point. When you bought the books from your packager, it probably charge a state sales tax. If if did, don't charge a sales tax when you resell the book. You don't have to charge or pay sales taxes on the resale of the book. If you do charge a sales tax, you're opening up another series of forms and regulations and quarterly tax statements. You don't want to go through that if you don't have to.

A second way to sell your book is via websites such as Smashwords, Kindle, Amazon, Barnes & Noble and others. Unlike the personal selling mention above, you won't meet the buyer or even know who he or she is, so you won't be able to thank them for buying your book.

A third way to sell books is via bookstores. Similar to the web selling, you won't know who purchased your book. Libraries may also purchase your book from their distributor.

Web selling and book store sales have one thing in common; when the book is sold, you don't get paid immediately. You will eventually, but you'll have to wait a while. Most packagers distribute royalties once a month. Before you can get paid, you'll have to set up channels that allow the packager to disburse the money to you. Some of the options include sending a check to your home, a PayPal deposit or a direct deposit to a bank account. These last two are known as Electronic Funds Transfer (EFT). Which option your packager wants you to use will be found somewhere on its website. If you want a check mailed to your home, the packager may specify that they won't disburse the funds until they exceed a hundred dollars whereas the EFT options don't have a minimum. Packagers will discourage you from selecting the physical check method: it's too much work for them and most packagers won't allow it.

PayPal

To use Paypal as your method of getting paid, you'll need to establish a Paypal account. Go to https://www.paypal.com. I suggest you label it as a business account rather than a personal account and use your business tax id number (if you have one) instead of your personal Social Security number. (See Chapter 9 for information on obtaining a tax id number).

Make sure your password is as strong as you can make it (while still remembering it). Your Paypal identification is the email address you put into your profile information. If people go to the Paypal website and type in your email address, they can deposit money to your account, but they can't withdraw funds from your account (that's a relief, isn't it?). You also have to provide information from a credit card to activate the account. More on that later.

As a business, Paypal provides you with a number of useful features.

If you sell books directly from your website, you can create a Paypal "buy now" button and install it on the web page   When visitors click on the 'buy now" button, they are taken to a Paypal page that collects the money. After that, the visitor can be taken to a page on your website with a download link or, a much better alternative, to a page that says "Thank You. The book you ordered will be attached to an email within twenty-four hours." Meanwhile, you will get an email from Paypal stating that a customer bought an item and deposited money into your account. You will also get the email address of the customer from Paypal.

Why use the "Thank you" email approach instead of a download link? After all, the download link is simpler; the customer can get the book immediately and you don't have to become involved. The purpose of sending the book as an attachment is to protect your book from hackers. If you put the book on your website as a downloadable pdf file, you'll have to 'hide' it so that visitors to the site can't see it and download a freebie copy. That's the theory, anyway. The reality is this: as long as the pdf file is on your site, web-savvy visitors will find it. They will prowl your site looking for downloadable stuff and grab whatever they can find even if they have no idea what it is they're downloading. For that reason it is better to keep your book's pdf file off the website and send it to the customer as an attachment.

In summary, don't put a downloadable pdf file on a website unless it's intended to be a free download.

You can also use Paypal to pay bills. As an example, my cover artist bills me using a Paypal feature. I get an email from Paypal stating that the cover artist has requested a payment of $YYY. The email has a link to Paypal where I can sign in and pay the bill directly from Paypal.

So, what if I don't have enough money in Paypal to cover the bill? Paypal will use the available money in the account and charge your credit card for the rest.

As an alternative to using the money in the account, you can elect to pay the entire bill with your credit card.

Paypal also allows you to link a bank account to your Paypal account. This can be used to transfer money between the bank and Paypal. The transfer works in both directions. If you have excess money in Paypal, you can transfer all or a portion of the money to the bank. If you don't have enough money in Paypal to cover a bill, the remainder will be taken from the linked bank account instead of being charged to your credit card. PayPal is very flexible.

Bank transfers

Packagers prefer to transfer your money directly to a bank account or to your PayPal account using the EFT process. To establish a bank transfer, you'll have to tell the packager the account's routing information and the account number. This information is found on the bottom of your checks. The packager will have a form for you to provide these routing and account numbers. They'll also have an explanation on where to find the appropriate numbers. Setting up a PayPal EFT process is similar.

Tax Information:

Your packagers will insist that you send them a signed W9 form. This is a tax form so the packager can provide information to the government on how much money they paid you in the year. Libraries and schools will also request this form if you give paid lectures or appearances. A blank W9 form can be downloaded from the IRS website.

You can take a blank W9 form, fill it out, sign it and then scan the form. This will produce a jpg file of the form that you can attach to an email. This process will negate the need to fill out the form for each organization that needs a copy, which you'd have to send by snail mail. Most organizations will accept this electronic version.

Print on demand

Unlike the other topics in this book, this one doesn't require you to do anything. It's simply an explanation of how packagers and many publishers operate.

Print on Demand, or POD as it is usually called, is a process that is used to fulfill print book orders. It is used extensively by the indie press houses and all the packagers you'll come across.

The way the traditional publishers operate is that they print thousands of books at one time and ship them to warehouses in advance of the book's release date. From there, the books are distributed to bookstores. This is an expensive way to do business and it only fits the business model of the big boys. The small publishers and packagers need a different business model and POD suits their needs perfectly.

In effect, what POD means is that copies of your print book don't physically exist until someone places an order for a copy. There are no shelves filled with your books waiting for someone to buy one. Once an order is received, the cover and manuscript files are printed, packaged and sent to the customer.

From a business perspective, the beauty of this system is there are no inventory costs and no warehouse costs. There are no problems with book returns, an issue that bugs the big publishers. Finally, there are no surplus books to be destroyed.

With modern computer-controlled printing machines, the POD book can be printed almost instantly. Most orders can be fulfilled within a day or two when placed in a book store if the packager is IngramSpark. If the packager is Kindle, the interval may be different.

Hire an Editor

Getting one or more editors to work on your book is not optional; it is a mandatory requirement! Editors provide another pair of eyes to read and polish your manuscript. You may think your manuscript is perfect, but it isn't. It doesn't matter how many times you went through it to dig out typos and to polish sentences, it still needs an editor.

There are four different types of editors: developmental, line, copy and proof readers. All four have quite different functions.

Developmental editors help with story line and character development and plot. These are the most expensive type of editor. If you use this type, it should have been done long before you started the publishing process.

Line editors provide comprehensive help and will look at plot, sentence structure, dialogue, word usage, and multiple other issues. Beta readers will do some of these functions, and if you have a competent team of them you most likely won't need this type of editor.

Copy editors will find a lot of mistakes you missed. These include typos, incorrect usage ('to' instead of 'too' or 'two'). A good editor will also find clumsy sentence structure, repeated words and other mistakes.

Proof readers are similar to copy editors. They will find typos, grammar and check for complete sentence and the occasional wrong word usage but don't really care about your clumsy sentences or bad dialogue.

At an absolute minimum, your book will require copy editing. If your errors are not rooted out, the reader will think she bought a book written by an amateur. If you want to produce quality content, it has to be professionally edited. Always remember, your name will be on the title page and the cover, so you want the book to be as perfect as possible.

If you don't know any editors, ask in one or two groups on LinkedIn. When you get a few names of editors, send them an email describing your project and ask for a price and when they can begin working on your manuscript. Most of them will quote a per-word cost or a per-page cost. This allows you to establish a price for the editing. Some editors will give you a flat rate. If you don't know the editor, be suspicious of this flat rate if it is much lower than the prices of editors who give a per-word or per-page price. The flat-rate editor may be giving you a low-ball price to get the business. Later on, you may get a message that the editing is more complicated than anticipated along with a demand for more money. In this instance, you could end up paying more than you would have with a per-word or per-page editor.

Editing will be the most expensive cost in your publishing process. Make sure you account for this in your budget.

You should get the editing underway now or even earlier if possible because it will take time for the editor to do her job, especially if she has other projects in front of yours.

The usual result of an editor's work is you end up with a manuscript that has a multitude of corrections that must be made. An alternative is to request the editor ship you each chapter when it is finished. This allows you to spread out the revision work over time.

One final word about editors: It's your book and you don't have to a accept everything the editor says. This is especially true if the editor wants to change the characters' dialog.

Marketing Tasks

Create a Web Page

Whether you like it or not, you're publishing your book in the twenty-first century and the way self-published books are found and bought these days is via the internet. Therefore, you and your book need a web presence.

The simplest way to establish a web presence is to use a program like Wordpress or Blogger or Weebly.

Blogger can be found at https://www.blogger.com/about/?r=2. It is an app from Google and is fairly simple to use but is limited in its flexibility. Wordpress is much more flexible. You can find Weebly at https://www.weebly.com

Wordpress comes in two versions. One, Wordpress.com, uses a Wordpress server that is common to many, many bloggers and the second, Wordpress.org, uses a server that you rent from a service provider. In this latter case, you have to decide on a host server and obtain a URL. More about these issues later on in this section.

The shared version of Wordpress uses a combined URL like http://wordpress/your name. The other version of Wordpress requires you to buy a URL to establish your own website. Whichever Wordpress version you use, you can build a complete website with it including a blog. My website hankquense.org/wp uses Wordpress. I use the second type of Wordpress, the one that isn't shared with others.

To get started with Wordpress, you'll have to select a template. Each template (and there are many of them) sets up your website. You'll have to browse through the templates to find one. My website uses the theme Adventurous. It has quite a few advanced features and I don't recommend it for someone who is putting together her first website.

Once the template is selected and installed you can move on to the plugin issue (Most servers will automatically install the template once you select it). Wordpress has hundreds (literally!) of plugins you can install into your website. The plugins are small dedicated programs designed to handle one or two functions. You'll only need a few plugins to start. I recommend Akismet Anti-spam. This plugin prevents spam comments from showing up on your website. You don't need the paid version of this plugin. I also recommend you install the Wordfence Security plugin. This one will provide you with a measure of protection from unauthorized logins and other attempts to compromise your website.

Websites such as Wordpress have two essential types of content: pages and posts. Pages are static in that they don't change unless you deliberately set out to change them. Once you establish a page on the website, it stays there, doesn't move and doesn't change.

Posts are for blogging and these aren't static like pages. A new blog post will appear at the top of the website once you publish it. When you write a second post, the initial one will move down to make room for the new post.

So how do you go about building a website? Here is how I put together my website http://hankquense.org/wp/. I used A Small Orange (ASO) https://asmallorange.com as my hosting server and I used them to establish the domain name. My domain name in this case is hankquense.org. When you put http:// in front of the domain name, you get a web link that is called a URL.

I recommend you use your author name for your domain instead of the book's title. If the domain name is your name, you are developing your brand. If it's the book's title, you'll need a second domain name for your new book whereas you can add any number of books to a domain that uses your author name.

Once you have the URL, you can set up a server service. Essentially what you do is rent a portion of the memory on a server. A server is a vast computer complex that serves many websites.

A Small Orange has a feature that allows you to painlessly establish a Wordpress site by clicking an option on a list of possible features.

So what do you do with a website once you have it up and running? You use it to pimp your book. There should be a dedicated page for the book and it should be easy to find. Don't make a visitor search for the book page.

Initially that page should have a picture of the cover, your book blurb and buy links. You can also put your short synopsis on it.

Use your blog to write blog posts. The blog posts can be about anything: your grandkids, your prison record (just kidding), writing anecdotes, vacation plans and pictures. The important thing is to issue blog posts periodically so that people will build up an interest in the blog and revisit it. It will be important to write blog posts about the book also. Tell the readers why you wrote the book, what problems you had to overcome, what you liked about the process. You can also interview your characters.

If this section doesn't make sense to you, I'd advise you to invest in a book on blogging. You may find one in your library, but check the publication date. If it was published a few years ago, it already has outdated information. Read a book that was published no more than a year ago.

An alternative to creating your own website is to share one with other authors. Typically, an author or a small company will put together the website and allow other authors to buy a listing on it. Each author gets a page to post about books, blurbs and bio information. The site also provides an individual URL and blogging ability. But see Book Seller Websites under Scams in Chapter 10.

One such shared site that I'm familiar with is run by my friend and fellow author Ed Charlton. It's called Author Showcase and you can find out more at: http://www.newauthorshowcase.com/.

If you join Ed's service, you'll get your own URL similar to this: author.is/yourname. You also get your own page and the ability to write blog posts.

No matter how you come about getting your website, once it's up and running, **_use it!_** Start writing blogs and post material about your book.

Before we leave this topic let's discuss website security. This issue is primarily associated with a stand-alone web site. It's a vital issue because of the proliferation of trolls and hijackers. These come in two flavors: bots and humans. Bots are small programs that cruise around the web and scan sites they come across. All bots are not evil. Search engines use them to build up their content. On my websites, I see a lot of bots (and humans) trying to access the site by logging in as an administrator. If they guess the correct user name and password, they'll be able to take control of the website and use it for their own purposes. If they also change the password, I'll be locked out of my own site and I'll have to contact the server support if this happens.

Another problem area is a bot or human installing malware on your site. This is a computer program that can infect other websites that contact your site.

The purpose of all this scary talk is to convince you to deploy website security programs. These programs can detect attempts to hijack or infiltrate your site and block the attempt. The security software has lists of URL's that it blacklists and will prevent those URL's from accessing your site.

I use the Wordfence plugin. It has a free version that provides a good level of protection and also gives you reports on who (or what) is accessing your site. If you think someone or something is suspicious, you can block them. The paid version ($100/year) provides a much great degree of protection. If you search for security plugins on Wordpress, you'll come across a number of highly rated ones. Almost all of them have a free version and a paid version.

Chapter 5: 3 Months Before Launch

Overview

You're now at three months before the launch date for your book. It's getting closer. At this point, there are a number of important tasks to be worked on.

However, most of these tasks overlap the publishing and the marketing projects and will have to be considered as part of each. For that reason, this chapter will be divided into a publishing task and a set of common tasks.

Publishing tasks:

- Establish the book price

Common tasks:

- Develop keywords
- Write a book blurb
- Write a synopsis

These tasks will be time-consuming and involve a bit of creativity along with some research.

Publishing Tasks

Establish the book price

How do you come up with a price for your book? I'll answer that in a moment. First, a few words of advice. Don't let your ego get in the way of making a rational decision on this subject. It's true you may have spent years producing this masterpiece and you think the book's value is enormous and that thousands of readers will be happy to pay a premium price to get a chance to own their very own copy. Well, you're wrong. You are an unknown author and unknown authors can't command premium prices. It'll be hard enough selling your book without the added burden of an unrealistically high price.

Back to the question on how to come up with the price. The answer is research. Let's consider print books first. The best place to do this research is on Amazon or some other major book site, although you can do this in a book store or even a library. Once on the site, search for books that are similar to yours. If your book is non-fiction and covers plumbing repairs, search for other plumbing repair books. Note the price for the ones that have similar subject matter and a similar number of pages. That is the target price of your book. If your research reveals four similar print books and their prices range from $15.99 to $24.99, your book should be priced somewhere within that range. You can also make a pricing decision to make your book available at a lower price if you wish.

If your book is fiction, search for other books within your genre. This may be a tougher job than with the non-fiction books. Genre books have superstar authors who command premium prices. Ignore them. You don't have the clout to demand a premium price — yet. Your search should be for lesser known authors in your genre. If your book has three-hundred pages, you should search for other similar genre books with three-hundred pages, approximately. Comparing your three-hundred page book to a six-hundred page one isn't very productive. The six-hundred page print book will cost more to produce because of the larger number of pages and subsequent production costs, so that book will require a higher price than a three-hundred page print book. Set your price to get the best possible sales at your current status as a new author.

For an ebook, the search process is similar but you'll probably come up with a confusing array of data. A bit of explanation is in order. There is a debate going on about ebook pricing. Many voices claim that ebooks sell best if they're priced at $0.99. Others contend that a higher price yields more profits but fewer sales. There are studies that conclude the sweet spot for an ebook is $2.99 to $5.99. Obviously, an ebook selling for $2.99 will bring in more revenue for an author that an ebook selling at $0.99. On the other hand, an ebook selling for $.99 could sell more books than a higher priced ebook. You can ask for advice on web sites like LinkedIn and you'll get replies, many of them contradictory. After reading the replies, it still comes down to you making a decision. Make sure this is a business decision.

Another complicating factor is the presence of best-selling authors. Their ebooks come from the major publishing houses. Their price will be closer to $10.00 or even higher. It will not even be close to $.99. Here again, the premium price is due to name recognition and clout. If you price your ebook close to $10.00 you won't have to worry about tracking sales; you won't get any. A first-time self-published author simply can't expect to use premium pricing and sell any books, no matter how great the content is.

Here is my pricing strategy. For my novels, I start out at $3.99 for ebook and $19.99 for print. As the book ages, I'll drop the ebook price lower.

For non-fiction, I initially price a multi-topic ebook at $4.49. Some of my non-fiction books are dedicated to a smaller topic and I price them at $2.99.

Common Tasks

Keywords

Keywords are frequently referred to as tags.

You may not be aware of this, but search engines don't care about your book title. It's true if you enter your title or your name into a search engine, the results will include your book and your name.

Readers will often search for a book using the name of a best-selling author but readers can't enter your title or name since you and your book have achieved little recognition so far.

Another way readers will search for a book is by using a short descriptive phrase such as 'fantasy quest' or 'regency romance'. This is the situation where you want your book to appear in the search results. To accomplish this, it is vital that you develop a set of keywords that will ensure your book title will show up in the reader's search results.

The keywords you want to use are ones that readers in your genre will use when browsing for a book. These keywords are not necessarily what your book is about: they are the terms a reader will type into a search engine. Let's say your book is a fantasy novel filled with elves and dwarfs. You may think 'dwarfs' and 'elves' would be great keywords. They are not. A reader looking for a fantasy novel won't use them, but instead will search on keywords like 'fantasy adventure' or 'fantasy quest.' Consequently, it is important for your marketing efforts that you develop a relevant set of keywords.

Google has a free keyword planner you can use to help generate your keywords. You can access it using this link: https://ads.google.com/home/tools/keyword-planner/

Another free keyword tool can be found here: https://keywordtool.io/

Here is a trick you can use on Amazon. In the search box, start to type a keyword. Amazon will auto-complete and show you its most popular keywords. As an example, type fantasy into the box. By the time you finish typing 'fantasy' you'll see some keywords that may be relevant. Keep typing and add the word 'adventure'. Now you'll see better keyword suggestions.

You'll have to develop your keywords before you upload your book to a packager (more on packagers later). If you have a publisher, they will develop the keywords for you.

Your keywords can also be used with blog posts about your book. On your blog posts there is space to enter all the keywords you developed. This will assist search engines in finding your blog post.

To repeat: keywords are important. Spend time to develop the correct set.

Once you get a set of keywords, you can use them in a variety of ways. Besides the packagers and blog posts, you can embed them into your book blurb and your short and long synopsis. Search engines love this usage.

As an example, here is the blurb for my new novel *The King Who Disappeared* before I generated the keywords: 'A long time ago, Bohan was a king. But that was before the sleep spell. Now that he's awake again, it's time for revenge.' (Book blurbs are the next topic.)

The keywords I used are: fantasy adventure, fantasy quest, fantasy humor, fantasy comedy .

Using these keywords, I modified the book blurb to: 'A long time ago, at the beginning of this *fantasy adventure*, Bohan was a king. But that was before the sleep spell. Now that he's awake again, it's time for a *quest* to get revenge. *Fantasy humor* doesn't get better than this.'

If you wish to get into keywords in depth, there is an excellent book on the subject called *How to Sell Fiction on Kindle* by Michael Alvear. It sells for $4.99 and is worth the price.

Book Blurbs

The purpose of the book blurb is to grab the attention of a potential reader. Once you have her attention by means of a great pitch line as the opening sentence, you need to follow that up with a few more sentences that tell her what's different about your book and what's in it for her.

Many new authors consider a book blurb to be a short synopsis. This is a mistake. Book blurbs and a short synopsis are two different animals and they have different purposes.

A book blurb is a marketing opportunity. The short synopsis is what goes on the inside cover flap on a hardcover book while the book blurb goes on the back cover. With a paperback, the blurb goes on the back cover.

In the case of an ebook, the blurb goes into the description on the book's web page. This can be followed by the short synopsis or reviews for your other books. The blurb can also go into the ebook before the title page so it will show up in a sample view.

Here are descriptions for each of the three elements involved in developing a book blurb. Some of the material you developed in your strategic marketing plan will be helpful here.

Pitch Line: This is the first statement and it is the hook to grab the reader's attention. Its purpose is to persuade the reader to keep reading the other two statements. It should be simple, one or two sentences at most, and it must make a clear statement about your book.

What's in it for the buyer? This is a statement that explains what the reader (i.e. a book buyer) will get in exchange for money. This must be explicit. This statement is not the place to get cute. Don't come across like the legendary used-car salesman. Tell the reader what benefit he'll get from buying the book. Think of this statement in this way; if your book is surrounded by hundreds of similar-sized books on a shelf in a bookstore, what would persuade the buyer to choose your book instead of one of the others?

What's different about this book? With all the books published every month, what makes your book stand out from the others?

The secret to creating an effective blurb is to keep rewriting and condensing it until it expresses the ideas with a minimum of words.

For example, this is the book blurb for my novel *Falstaff's Big Gamble*.

Pitch Line: This novel is Shakespeare's Worst Nightmare.

What's in it for the buyers? It takes two of the Bard's most famous plays, Hamlet and Othello, and recasts them into a fantasy land called Gundarland. There, Hamlet becomes a dwarf and Othello a dark elf

What's different about this book? If that isn't bad enough, these two tragedies are now comedies with Falstaff, Shakespeare's most popular rogue, thrown in as a bonus.

For my non-fiction how-to book *Planning a Novel, Script or Memoir*, I developed this blurb.

Pitch Line: Creating a long story such as a novel requires a great deal of effort and creativity. It is easy to get lost in details and to lose focus on the main issues.

What's in it for the buyers? This book describes a process to plan the work prior to writing the first draft. The purpose of the plan is to allow the author to concentrate on the important elements of the story.

What's different about the book? A major portion of the book describes a method of developing a roadmap to keep the writer on target. The plan can be used to develop any long story such as a novel, a script, a memoir or even a play.

Here is a tongue-in-cheek blurb for a memoir.

Pitch Line: I really only wanted to study math, but I ended up ruling the world.

What's in for the buyers? I reveal my secret to manipulate the markets and gain control of a commodity and possibly the world.

What's different about the book? I tell my story of how, after getting advanced degrees in math and computer science, I dabbled in the stock market and cornered the market for Stanislite, the rare mineral that gives superheroes their unique powers, thus gaining control over the superheroes.

When you use your blurb, don't use the term "pitch line" or the questions. Just have the statement flow into a short paragraph. When you develop your blurb, incorporate your book's keywords. This technique will improve your search engine results.

So what are blurbs good for other than what was discussed above? How else can they be used? You can use them anywhere they'll fit. If you can't fit the entire statement someplace (such as on *Twitter*), use the pitch line by itself.

Here are some other common uses.

On a website: On your book-buying web page or in a blog post, make the pitch line the opening statement followed by the rest of your blurb. Why? On the internet, attention spans are too minuscule to measure. When visitors land on your web page, you have a second or two to persuade them to read beyond the first line of text they see. That is the job of your pitch line: to get the visitors to read the rest of the blurb.

Book Trailers: Make sure your blurb statements are clearly visible and emphasized in the trailer. Get the message in the beginning and the end of the trailer. Innumerable people from all over the world may view the trailer and you want them to understand your message.

Internet Announcements: Log onto social media sites and post an announcement that your book will be or is available. Include the blurb in the opening part of the announcement. Use it on book sites like Goodreads. After the blurb, add information about your book. You can upload the cover image and add descriptive text about it.

Press Releases: Display your blurb prominently. Make it the opening statement in the body of the release. Rephrase it and place it a second time further down in the body.

Sig Files: Use the signature capability in your email program to build a unique signature using the pitch line by itself. Link that pitch line to a book-seller website. Now, every time you send an email, you'll also be pitching your book. Sig files are discussed in Chapter 6.

Write a Synopsis

From Wikipedia: *"The definition of a synopsis is: a brief summary of the major points of a written work, either as prose or as a table; an abridgment or condensation of a work"*.

Once you've written the book, you have to shrink it down into a manageable chunk that will allow others to digest what the book is about without investing a major amount of time on it.

You need two versions of the synopsis, a long one and a short one. Generally speaking, the shorter a synopsis is, the harder it is to write.

The long synopsis should be a few pages. It's what agents and book publishers will want to see if you're inclined to go down that path. Another purpose is to accompany queries sent to book review sites and bloggers. This allows the potential reviewer to get a good idea about the book so she can determine if it's a book she wants to read and review. It also goes into your media kit. (See Chapter 6)

Write the long one first, then edit, edit and edit it again until it is shrunk down to the short version.

The short synopsis should be less than a single page. Think about that for a minute. You wrote a book. Let's say it's eighty thousand words long. Now you have to describe it in a few paragraphs? Perhaps three hundred words?

I'll make an observation on writing the short synopsis; it's a challenge to chop down your entire book into a few paragraphs. However, it's necessary. No matter how tough it is, do it. Fellow author Dale Lehman has written an excellent article on writing a short synopsis which he calls the 'cover blurb:' https://writingcooperative.com/the-cover-blurb-711549b30a5a

Many authors consider writing a synopsis the toughest part of creating a book. Some think the short synopsis is a tougher chore than writing the book.

The short synopsis has many uses, many more uses than the longer version. It can go on your website as part of the book page. It can also be used in blog posts and in emails. This short synopsis is frequently found on the inside cover flap on hard-bound editions. For paperbacks, the short synopsis is often found on the back cover after the book blurb.

On my cover shown in Chapter 3, the back cover has the blurb followed by reviews for some of my previous novels. Whether to use the short synopsis or reviews is yet another decision a self-publishing author has to make.

No matter what tense the book is written in, synopses are written in the present tense, not past tense. Why? I don't know. Maybe it's tradition. Never mind why, just make sure you write it in the present tense.

Chapter 6: 2 Months Before Launch

Overview

With two months to go before launch, the number of tasks increases in both the publishing and marketing phases of the project. Unlike the other chapters, the tasks listed in this chapter are to be completed during the two month time frame leading up to the launch date.

Under publishing, it's time to prep the manuscript for uploading to packagers. You remember packagers, right? We discussed them way back in Chapter 4. It's time to dig out those website locations and prepare to use them.

With the marketing, it's time to start telling people about the book and to begin the never-ending quest for book reviews. That's right! Even though you have done some marketing before now, your marketing campaign is about to kick into high gear.

The publishing tasks covered in this chapter are:
- Revise the manuscript
- Format the book
- Complete the book design
- Get an ISBN
- Upload to the packagers
- Get advanced review copies

The marketing tasks are:
- Get a trailer
- Create an Amazon Central page

- Start social media campaigns
- Initiate Goodreads reviewer requests
- Start an email list
- Create an email signature
- Commission a blog tour

Publishing tasks

Revise the Manuscript

By now you should have the marked-up manuscript back from the editor. Make all the suggested corrections (the ones you agree with) and come up with the final draft of the manuscript. This is the version you will use to format the book for uploading to the packager.

If the editor suggests wholesale revisions or rewrites, you may have to consider pushing the launch date out further. Remember, you don't have to accept everything the editor tells you to change. The editor is making suggestions and you have the freedom to reject them.

Format the book

This topic contains a lot of technical detail and is longish. I've organized it using bullet items.
- Print & ebook versions
- Print book formatting
- Ebook formatting

- Epub3 requirements
- Embedded links

Print & Ebook Versions

If you plan to publish both an ebook and a print book, you'll have to format two different versions of your manuscript. And the versions will be quite different.

No matter how many versions you need, I suggest you make a digital copy of the final revision of the original manuscript and put it away someplace safe. Call this version your master manuscript. Work with copies of it to format the different versions of your book.

If you format a file for a print book and then upload it to an ebook packager, you will end up with an ebook that is mostly unreadable. In the case of the Smashwords packager, your file will be instantly rejected because of incorrect formatting. Similarly, a file formatted for an ebook and sent to a print packager will result in a mess.

Print Book Formatting:

Formatting the print book is straight forward. Make sure you use a copy of the master manuscript for this task, not the master itself.

Your word processor assumes whatever you wrote will be printed so the program's default settings support a print edition. What you see on the computer screen is pretty much what the print book will look like.

The biggest chore right now is to ensure the manuscript is uniform. Review it and correct any inconsistencies. With that done, you're ready to move on to the print book layout task. This topic is discussed later in this chapter.

Ebook Formatting:

This task is radically different from the print book formatting. Much of the work here comes about because your word processor is set up for document printing. Many of those pesky defaults are not acceptable for ebooks, which have to be formatted in accordance with the Epub3 Standard. Other than Kindle, there are few, if any, packagers who will accept an uploaded file that isn't Epub3 compliant.

Use another copy of the master manuscript file to develop the ebook manuscript.

To begin the formatting, eliminate the headers and footers. This will, of course, eliminate your page numbers. One aspect of ebooks is that page numbers become irrelevant because e-readers can adjust the type of font and the size of the font. This ability to change fonts makes page numbers extraneous. Any page numbers you see in an ebook reader were added by that ebook reader software.

Next, eliminate all page breaks and replace them with three blank lines. Ebooks can't have page breaks so if your master manuscript had a page break after the end of each chapter, the page break has to be replaced. If you don't remove the page breaks, they will be eliminated by the packager's software, and that can lead to unpredictable results.

That takes care of the easy part.

Epub3 Requirements

The Epub3 Standard has rigid requirements and ebook packagers such as iBooks, Barnes & Noble and Smashwords demand adherence to the standard. Kindle doesn't require this adherence, which accounts for the poor quality found in many ebooks published by Kindle. As an aside, the books published the 'Lazy Way' are published by Kindle, not by packagers who follow the Epub3 Standard.

Fortunately, there is an excellent book on how to format an ebook in accordance with the Epub3 Standard. It's called the *Smashwords Style Guide* and its author is Mark Coker, the Smashwords founder and president. It's a free download and you can download a copy here: https://www.smashwords.com/books/view/52

Most writers have developed habits that violate the Epub3 Standard, and these violations have to be corrected before uploading the file to a packager. To find these violations, you have to turn on a formatting guide built into all word processors. These are called invisibles or non-printing characters and can be turned on or off by a selection in the toolbar at the top of the word processor page. It is usually found under 'view' or 'format'. Each word processor does this a little differently so you may have to search for this software switch.

The invisibles usually are blue characters on a Mac and the image below shows some of them.

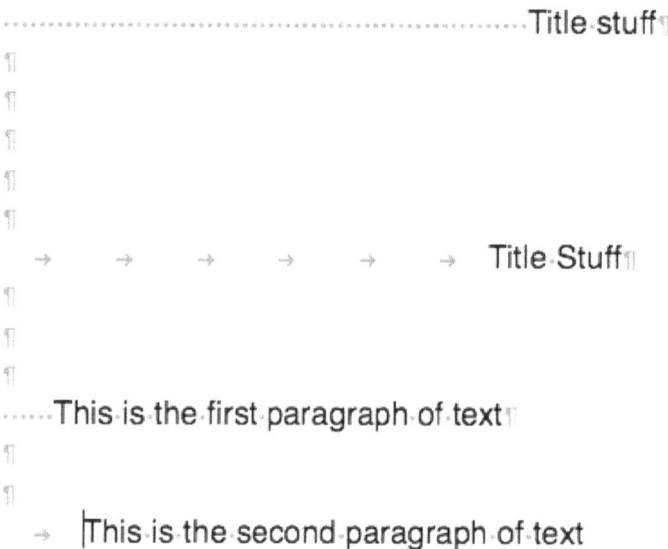

Each blue dot represents a space bar usage and the arrow is displayed when the tab key is used. The symbol that looks like a backward P is a carriage return or enter key.

If you used the tab key or space bar to center the chapter headings, this violates the Epub3 Standard, and they have to be removed and replaced by the center command. This command is usually found on the tool bar and looks like this:

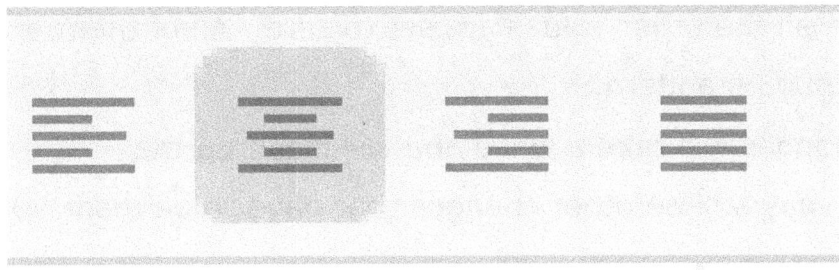

Indenting the first line of a new paragraph by using the space bar or the tab key is also a violation of the standard. These violations have to be removed (**_ALL_** of them!) and replaced by using the indent command. This is harder to find than the center command and it's usually found under the Format heading.

In Mac's word processor Pages, it's found in the inspector under Format, Layout, Indents. Here you can set up the indent for the first line of a new paragraph in quarter-inch increments.

In Open Office (a Word look-alike) it is found under Format, Paragraph and it opens a screen that looks like this:

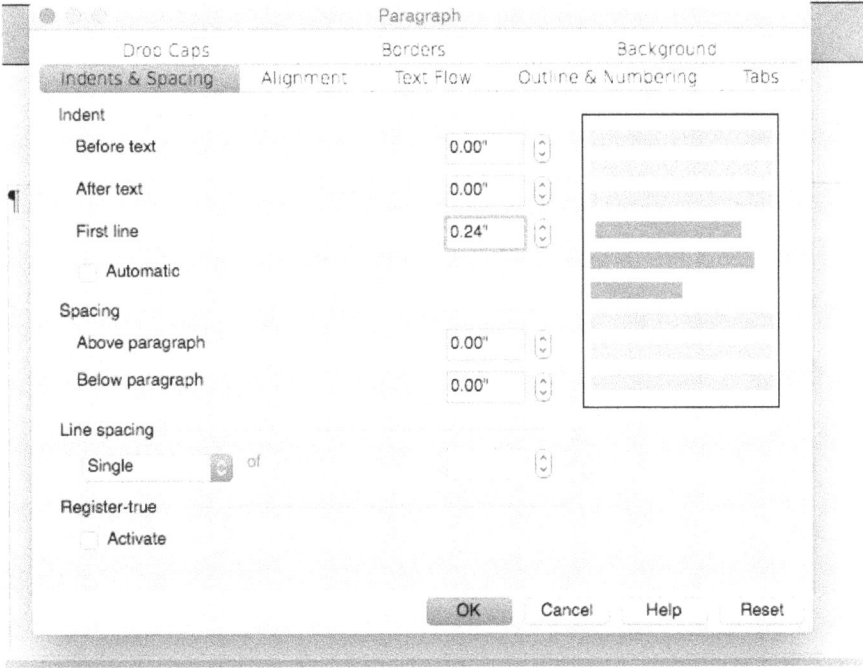

You can set the indent at First line to any value you wish. While you're on this screen, make sure all the other values are set to zero. All of them, if not zero, violate the Epub3 standard.

Making all these changes will take a while and will clean up the manuscript, but there may still be other changes that have to be made. Use the *Style Guide* to find them.

Still another task involves the Table of Contents. It has to be hyperlinked to the appropriate place in the manuscript. (Did I mention before that the Epub3 Standard was written for the readers, not the authors?) What this means is that if a reader clicks or touches Chapter 3 in the Table of Contents, the reader will instantly jump to the start of Chapter 3.

In brief, the way you establish these hyperlink jumps is to go through the manuscript and bookmark each chapter heading. Back in the Table of Contents, you then establish a hyperlink from the chapter listing to the associated bookmark. The *Smashwords Style Guide* has much more detail on this topic.

Your packager ***may*** hyperlink the Table of Contents, but there is no guarantee the packager will do it correctly. I prefer to do it myself and test each link to ensure it works properly.

Embedded Links

With an ebook, you can embed a link into the text like this: my website. When reader click or touch the link, they will go to the website behind the link. This scheme doesn't work with print books. Here you have to display the link like this: my website can be found at http://hankquense.org/wp/.

In this case, the reader will have to type the link into a browser search box or address bar.

Complete the Book Design

Book design refers to the layout of the interior of the book. Print books and ebooks will have different layouts, but most of this section deals with print books.

Print Book Design

With print books, your big decision is to decide on the size of your published book. If you go to a library or bookstore and look around, you'll see that the books come in a variety of sizes. Your book packager will allow you to select the book size from more a than dozen different sizes. My paperback books are 5.5 inches by 8.5 inches. Why? No special reason. It seemed like a good size when I published my first book and subsequent books are the same size so they match on a book shelf.

Once you decide on a size, you need to change the print master file pages to that size and establish margins on the top, bottom and both sides.

In Pages (for Macs), you'll find that command under Inspector, Document Inspector, Page Setup. In OpenOffice, the command is Format, Page, then enter the height and width you want.

With the size issue out of the way, you can now deal with margins. The left side (inside) margin will have to be different than the right side margin because of the spine and cover. For instance, if your book has between 151 and 400 pages, the left (inside) margin has to be .375 inches while the right (outside) margin must be at least .25 inches but can be greater. The margins can be set on the word processor page used to establish the page size.

Once you've changed the book size, you'll notice the book has changed significantly. Not the least of the changes is the number of pages has increased possibly appreciably. Make a note of the page count. You'll need this number to calculate the spine width.

The size change can have an impact on the book layout. For instance, if you started each chapter on a new page, you may find there is now a blank page or two in the book and you'll have to make adjustments to remove them.

Kindle has a help page on cover design with information on spine calculations. You can find it at: https://kdp.amazon.com/en_US/help/topic/G201857950. Provide your cover artist with this spine width measurement so he can produce a properly sized cover for your book. Don't do the spine width calculations until you finish the rest of the book design. Your choices can change the number of pages in the print book.

Other Design Concerns

One of the basic decisions you'll make is the font that you'll be using. There are many font families to choose from, and which one you use is a personal decision. I generally use Verdana font. That's the type used for this book (unless you changed it on an ebook reader). I also like Lucida Grande. Choosing a font can have economic repercussions for print books. Some fonts need more space than other fonts. The more space a font uses, the more pages a book will have. More pages means higher production costs. In other words, you, the publisher, have to balance the attractiveness of the font with the costs of producing a copy of the book.

In similar fashion, the size of the font used also affects the production costs. Obviously, a twelve point font will require more pages than a ten point font will. If you go for a small font size to lower production costs, you start to affect the readability of the book. Is the type so small that some potential readers won't buy it because they can't read it?

With ebooks, the font family and font size are mostly irrelevant. Once a reader has the ebook on her tablet, she can change the font family and the font size to suit her own tastes.

Line spacing is another parameter that can affect the number of print pages. No matter what spacing you use to write the book, either double-space or one-and-a-half space, change it to single space. This is the accepted standard for print books.

Chapter headings generally are a larger font than the text font. It is essential that all chapter headings use the same font and font size. Here is another question to ponder. How are your chapters handled? Does the next chapter start after three blank lines? (use this choice with the ebook edition.) Or do you use a page break to start a new page? Whatever you decide, be consistent throughout the book.

With headers and footers, use one or the other. I use only headers. That's where the page number goes and you can put the book's title there if you wish. Ebooks don't use (or allow) headers and footers so this is another print book only issue.

Front matter is material that is placed after the title page and contains copyrights and "do not reproduce notices" and so forth. It also lists the ISBN number and the packager's name.   This is also where you can put acknowledgements and dedications.

Cheat Sheets

To ensure the crucially important uniformity of my book design, I write everything down on a sheet of paper, essentially a cheat sheet. This is so I don't inadvertently change stuff in the middle of the book. The cheat sheet has the font family (Verdana in this book), the size of chapter headings (eighteen point), section size (fourteen point), the size of the text (twelve point), how many spaces between chapters (three lines), the spaces between sections (two spaces) and any other design information I need.

A cheat sheet will help ensure the book details are uniform.

Get an ISBN

ISBN stands for International Standard Book Number. Older books have a 10 digit ISBN number and new ones are assigned a 13 digit number. An ISBN is unique to a particular book and edition. Once an ISBN is assigned to your book, the number identifies your book in data base searches. If you do a book search on your ISBN from the other side of the galaxy, your book will show up as a result of the search. No other book has your ISBN.

Different versions of a book need different ISBN numbers. Hardcover and paperback editions use two different numbers. A paperback and an ebook edition have two different numbers. An audiobook edition uses still another ISBN.

Do You Need One?

While it's technically true that a book doesn't have to have an ISBN, bookstores (think Barnes & Noble and iBooks), libraries and some websites won't sell the book if it doesn't have an ISBN. Thus, the absence of an ISBN can severely limit the author's options.

An odd fact about ISBNs is that Kindle ebooks don't require one. Kindle only distributes its ebooks within the Amazon universe. This means they don't deal with bookstores or libraries and hence don't need an ISBN. Kindle will assign a number to your ebook that looks suspiciously like an ISBN but is called an ASIN. That stands for Amazon Standard Identification Number. For print books, Kindle will assign the standard ISBN if you let it.

Getting An ISBN

In the USA, ISBNs only come from a company called Bowker. Its website is here: http://www.bowker.com. The company has a monopoly on the issuance and registration of the ISBNs in this country.

How does an author acquire an ISBN for a book? This question has several possible answers. Many packagers such as Kindle (for print books) and Smashwords (for ebooks) will issue a free ISBN to authors who use those sites to distribute their books. Other packagers will charge the author a fee to assign an ISBN to the book. With some packagers, the author must provide the ISBN. This is the case with IngramSpark. If a packager charges you for an ISBN and the fee is more than a few dollars, you're getting ripped off.

If you have to or want to provide your own ISBN, you'll have to buy it from Bowker if you're in the USA, and it will cost you $125 for a single ISBN. I have a publishing company and I buy ISBNs in packages of ten. That lowers the price to $29.50 each. I do this because my publishing company is registered with Bowker, and the ISBNs I'm issued have my company's identification built into the ISBN. This identification is built into digits 6 through 10 of the ISBN number. These numbers identify the ISBN as issued to Strange World Publishing Company.

Packagers like Smashwords buy ISBNs in bundles of a thousand, and this reduces the price to a dollar or two each. This means if you accept a free ISBN from Smashwords, the number identifies Smashwords, not you, as the publisher. The Smashwords official wording with the ISBN reads like this: "Published by (your name) at Smashwords 2018."

Unless you plan to start your own publishing company, this issue isn't anything to lose sleep over.

There is one complication about an ISBN assigned to your book by Smashwords or other packager or with a Kindle print book. If you take your book and move to a different packager, you need a new ISBN. You can't continue to use the ISBN assigned by Smashwords or Kindle; they bought it, not you, and it's their ISBN. It's yours to use as long as your book is distributed by them.

Upload to Packagers

Before you can upload your files to a packager, you first have to establish an account with it.

Uploading to the packager doesn't have to be done at this stage, but it may be advisable to get it out of the way. Just because you uploaded it doesn't mean it will be available for sale immediately. You can dictate the date that the book goes on sale. One advantage of doing this early is that it will appear on the packager's website as a pre-order and you can start marketing it by referring to the website page. If you wish, you can postpone this step until much closer to the launch date, but if this is your first time publishing a book, doing it early will give you time to deal with any obstacles or problems that may crop up.

The next step is to read the packager's submission guidelines. They'll be different for each packager. An important piece of data is what format the manuscript must be in. Some will require a doc file, others will request a pdf file. Epub files are also a consideration. Make sure you upload the correct format or your file will be rejected. Cover files also require some checking.

For an ebook cover, most packagers want a jpg or png format but some require jpg only. For print books, the full wrap cover (as it's called) should be in pdf format.

After you start the process, you'll run into screens looking for more information about the book. These screens will have text boxes for the price, the keywords (or tags) and the ISBN number (if you're furnishing it).

With some packagers, you'll also run into offers to provide a number of optional services that will require money. These include formatting the book, doing the book layout, or designing the cover. If you don't have the computer skills or the time to do these tasks yourself, you may want to use the packager's services. Be advised that these services use premium pricing. You can probably get the same service at a lower price elsewhere. Ask on Goodreads and LinkedIn for recommendations.

You may also run into a screen that covers distribution options. Smashwords, for instance, has a premium option. With it, your book will be made available to Barnes & Noble, iBooks, Kobo and many more ebook sellers. While the option is free (and you should use it), it requires stringent adherence to the Epub3 standard. Smashwords may publish a book and sell it on its own website even if the book doesn't adhere completely to the Epub3 standard. Just because a book is accepted by Smashwords doesn't mean it will be accepted for premium distribution.

Get Advanced Review Copies

Advanced Review Copies (or ARCs) are a great boon to getting early reviews besides being an opportunity to catch a few additional typos. Once you get ARCs, you can offer them to book reviewers to read before the book becomes available. Getting them is a bit tricky depending upon who your ebook packager is. If you use Smashwords to package and distribute your ebook, you can download an ebook in pdf, epub and mobi formats at any time. You are then free to give out copies of these as you see fit.

If your packager is Kindle, the situation is quite different. You have one chance to get a copy and it will only be in mobi format.

Your only chance to get the mobi copy happens when you upload the manuscript to Kindle. At some point in the process, you will be asked if you wish to review the ebook file on your computer. Answer yes and Kindle will send a mobi edition to your computer for your review. This is your Kindle ARC and it's the only one you will get from Kindle unless you upload a revised copy (or pretend to upload a review copy and merely re-upload the original file).

Having only a mobi version limits your ability to engage with reviewers who need an epub or pdf edition. There are websites that offer to convert a mobi edition to other formats such as epub. The sites offer the reverse also: epub to mobi. Many of theses sites will require an account to use it and some require a subscription. One site you can use free is https://www.zamzar.com.

With print books, you'll be required to order one and review it before it will be become available for sale. You will then have to approve it or send a revised manuscript. Unlike ebooks, you will be charged production and mailing costs. However, if you are confident the book is good shape, you can order more than a single copy. These then become your Advanced Review Copies.

Marketing Tasks

Get a Trailer

Trailers are short movie-like films about your book. They are designed to educate, entice and entertain viewers. When you watch TV, you are constantly bombarded by trailers for movies and TV shows, so you have definitely seen trailers; you can't escape them.

If your marketing budget supports developing a trailer, now is the time to work on getting one.

Trailers can be expensive if you hire a top-notch production company to put one together for your book. Think $1,000 or more. With advances in software and competition, many production companies now produce trailers for a modest fee, generally less than $100. These less expensive trailers can be just as effective as the more expensive ones. You can do a web search to find trailer production companies, but you can also ask on LinkedIn and Goodreads.

You can also make a trailer yourself. I do. Granted, my trailers aren't as classy as the ones put out by a production company, but mine get the book's message out. I have more on DIY trailers in Chapter 10

If you make or commission a trailer, put it on your webpage as well as YouTube and add a link to it in your blog posts. You can also add the YouTube trailer link in tweets.

Amazon Central Author Page

Once your book is available for sale or pre-order on Amazon, you can start an Author Page. You'll find Author Central at: https://authorcentral.amazon.com/gp/home

After you login with your password, you can add your bio and other information to the page. One of the great features of the Author Page is you can add a wealth of information about the book that you couldn't do when you uploaded it to Kindle.

The book topics include *Editorial Reviews*. These are reviews that Amazon won't allow to be posted on the book site because Amazon won't allow paid reviews. If you receive a review from a prestigious site like *Publishers Weekly,* this is the place to post it.

Another topic is *From the Author*. Here you tell readers why you wrote the book. Or the problems you encountered in writing it. Or anecdotes from the writing process.

You can also upload videos to the page (i.e. a trailer) and you can set up an RSS feed so your blog posts show up on the Author Page.

Taken together, the Author Page is a great marketing tool.

A FAQs page about Author Central can be found at: https://authorcentral.amazon.com/gp/help?ie=UTF8&topicID=200799660

I suggest you make the Author Page link part of your email signature. Email signatures will be discussed later in this chapter.

Media Kit

The purpose of a media kit is to let folks in the media and other interested parties know about your writing credentials. If the book is your only writing project so far, there won't be a lot of material, but start it anyway. If you published short stories, articles or other material, add it to plump up your resumé.

The media kit lives on your website or blog and must be available to anyone who wants to download it. For that reason, you may want to consider not putting personal information in it like your home address, or your phone number.

So, what goes into a media kit? Here is a list of items that make up your kit:

- Bio.
- Press releases.
- Website links.
- Body of work.
- Book descriptions.
- Book reviews.

Make sure the media kit is a doc or pdf file so it can be downloaded and opened by everyone.

As long as we're discussing the media kit contents, it's a good time to write your bio. Write two bios, a long one of several pages and a short one, a single paragraph or two. The long one goes in the media kit and the short one can be used in guest posts on blogs and in other places.

Bios are written in third person, not first person. Include your photo in the bio and make sure it's a good picture. Preferably, you should be smiling. Don't use a picture in which you are frowning, glaring, snarling or otherwise looking unfriendly or hostile. You don't want to scare away potential customers.

Start Social Media Campaigns

Now is the time to start telling the world about your book. The way to do it is, of course, using social media. By now, you have created accounts on a few sites and are familiar with them. You also should have joined a few groups of other authors or readers. Hopefully, you have also participate in conversations and expressed your opinion or support.

I mostly use Facebook, Twitter, LinkedIn, Goodreads and blog posts. There are many other possibilities, like Pinterest, but I have never been able to get into using them. They just don't grab my interest or are too superficial. You'll have to select the ones that suit you.

Besides tweeting, I use my blog posts to spread the word by using links that connect the post to my social media sites. Thus, if I write a post describing my new book or containing an extract from a novel, the post is sent to Facebook, Twitter and LinkedIn by pushing buttons rather than copying and pasting the post.

Among the more useless things you can do on social media is to post material that essentially says, 'Buy my book'. This is the sign of an amateur and is considered offensive by many users. After you're on social media for a while, you'll be amazed at how many posts like this you'll see.

One approach to introducing the book is to use your book blurb and the cover in tweets and posts. Ensure that the post has a buy link in it. You can reissue the post weekly or even at shorter intervals.

While you are on your social media sites, look for material from other bloggers. Check out their sites to see if they are a fit for your book. What does this mean? Well, if the blogger writes about and reviews romance novels, don't contact her about your Vietnam War thriller. However, if the site features adventure stores, contact the blogger and ask if you can furnish a guest post about your book. Bloggers generally love guests. The guest post usually includes your brief bio, a mug shot and a cover image. In other words, it's a great way to promote your book.

You can also ask the bloggers if they're willing to review your book. If so, send them an ebook copy and a 'thank you' note. Don't be a total amateur and send the blogger a link to where she can purchase a copy.

Goodreads Review Requests

One great feature about Goodreads is that there are millions of readers on it. And those readers love to get free books to read and review. There are a number of groups that actively seek authors looking for reviews.

One such group is called *Advanced Copies for Review & Book Giveaways*. Here is a link to it: https://www.goodreads.com/group/show/58575-advanced-copies-for-review-book-giveaways.

A second group is: *Authors and Reviewers:* https://www.goodreads.com/group/show/103713-authors-reviewers.

There are more such groups on Goodreads, but these are the two that I have used to get book reviews.

When you request a review (your book must be on Goodreads), use your book blurb. You can also use your short synopsis. If group members are interested in your book, they will leave a message for you.

Browse these groups and read the review requests. If you see a book that sounds interesting, request a copy. Interactions like this increase your exposure within the group and the other author may return the favor of a review.

Email List

Email lists are a way to keep in touch with readers who have shown an interest in your books or your blog posts or your articles. You can maintain connect with these readers by sending out newsletters and updates on your newest book project.

Even though you haven't published your book yet, it isn't too early to start collecting emails.

To manage my email lists, (I have several) I use Mailchimp: www://mailchimp.com. It enables you to put together professional looking emails and newsletters. It will also give you amazing stats such as who opened the email and how many recipients clicked on links in the newsletter.

So how do you go about building an email list? Here is excellent article by a top-notch book marketer: https://www.janefriedman.com/email-newsletter-growth/.

Here is another good article, this one by Mailchimp. It discusses adding a signup form to capture important contact data for your list: https://mailchimp.com/help/add-a-signup-form-to-your-website/.

Spend time managing your list and remove anyone who requests it. Not removing those names means you'll be spamming them with future emails.

Email Signature

Now is a good time for you to develop a sig file. Email signatures (usually called sig files) are a free way to publicize your book every time you send out an email. Think about how many times a day that happens!

Sig files are those links you see beneath the name of the person who sent you the email. Here is what yours could look like:

Your name

Title of your book

Location of your website

The last two lines would be linked to a webpage, the first to a book buying page like Amazon, the second to your blog page.

Sig files are easy to implement and only take a few minutes. For the Mac mail program, open mail, click on preferences and then on signatures. This will open a new screen like the one shown below.

#

On the left is a list of your email accounts (if you have more than one). The middle column lists the signatures you have established. Right now, it's probably blank. Click on the (+) button and type a file name, such as 'sig 1'. In the right column, you can add the sig files you want and they will be linked to the sig name. To do this, type the name of your book in the right column, highlight the book name, right click on the mouse and click on 'link' and then type or paste the URL of your book page. Close the screen and every time you send out a new email, the link to your book's page will go with it.

With Gmail, go to the settings page and scroll down to Signature. There you'll see a text box to add whatever you want appended to your signature. You can add links as you need them. Other email programs will have a similar process to build a sig file.

If you use Outlook, this link will provide information about sig files in that program: https://www.mail-signatures.com/articles/outlook-email-signature-location-and-backup/

Commission a Blog Tour

Blog tours are an optional marketing task. Whether you use one or not depends on your marketing budget. If you can afford it, a blog tour is a good way to get many people (i.e. potential buyers) to learn about your book.

Here is an explanation of a blog tour from Penguin Random House:

A blog tour is a set amount of time, usually a week or two, in which your book will be promoted across various websites and blogs. The dates are set in advance; each blog knows what material it will be posting, and the content should be unique to each blog.

Blog tours are not the same as writing blog posts for your own blog. In a blog tour, you are a guest on other peoples' blogs. Blog tours are usually set up by a company who specializes in these tours and who have a lot of blogger contacts. You can set one up yourself if you have a number of blogger contacts, but it will require a lot of effort to contact the bloggers and schedule the acceptances.

If you sign up for a blog tour, expect to pay a chunk of money for it. Refer to the budgeting information in Chapter 1. You will also have to invest a substantial block of time working on it. For instance, if the tour encompasses ten stops (i.e. blog sites), you may have to prepare ten separate blog posts, and these blog sites expect original material, not cut and paste exercises.

Some of the bloggers' requests will include:
- An author interview. The blogger will generally provide a list of questions to answer
- A scene or two from the book
- Answers to a list of questions
- A post on why you wrote the book and any problems you ran into

To get a blogger to review your book, you'll have to furnish them with a copy. If you gave a copy to the tour operator, the company will furnish the book to the reviewer. Some bloggers won't review an ebook, only a print book.

The tour company will establish a list of sites you'll visit and a date for each one. Your tour will usually take place over a period of two to four weeks depending upon how many stops you'll be making.

You can find blog tour operators by searching on the web. You can also ask other writers about their experiences with various operators. Use your LinkedIn groups for this research. Typically, once you sign up and pay, you'll be assigned a tour guide who will answer your questions, find the appropriate bloggers and establish dates for the tour.

Here is one caveat about blog tours. It won't do much good if the blog stops aren't appropriate for the book you wrote. If you wrote an adventure story, don't get involved with blog tour operator who specializes in romance blog tours, even if the price is reasonable. In this case, you'll have wasted your money because the visitors to your blog stops will have no interest in your book.

If you decide to use a blog tour, this is the time to set it up and start organizing the material. Schedule it so you'll be bouncing around the blogs before, during and after the launch. I prefer the tours to start one week before the launch date.

Once your tour begins, take advantage of the chance to broaden your social media reach. In the post's comment section, add a thank you note. Check on the site several times to see if any visitors posted a comment. If they did, respond to it, politely and positively. Save the link to the blogger's site. It's valuable information and use it to check the site occasionally and post comments if appropriate.

You should be aware that some blog tour operators are scammers. Before committing to a blog tour, ask the operator for the contact information of a few customers. If the tour is legitimate, you'll get a few names and email addresses. If the tour operator replies that the customer information is confidential, the tour most likely is a scam operation. Flee! For more information on blog tour scammers see Chapter 10.

I'm familiar with two legitimate blog tours. Mason Canyon is on the inexpensive side, around $200-300. For more information, go to https://mcbooktours.com. Author Marketing Experts is top-notch and expensive, more than a $1,000. Here is a link to the website: https://www.amarketingexpert.com.

Chapter 7: Launch

Overview

It's finally here: Launch Day! This is the day the unsuspecting world awakes to discover your book is now available. But no one knows about it except possibly your family and friends.

If you want more people to know about the book, you have to tell them.

Under publishing, there is only one final task that has to be done before the publishing part of the project is complete.

Marketing is another story. Probably to your dismay, I have to tell you marketing never ends. It just goes on and on *ad nauseam* as long as the book is available. On the other hand, I know authors who relish the challenge of marketing their books. Perhaps you're one of that plucky band of book marketeers.

The marketing tasks covered in this chapter are:
- Newsletter
- Press release
- Web announcements
- Blog tour sites

Publishing Tasks

Celebrate!!!!!

Have a beer. Wait, have two beers. Go out to dinner.

Then start marketing the book.

Marketing Tasks

Newsletter

If you've completed the previous marketing tasks, you'll have a list of email addresses of people who are interested in your book. You may also have a Mailchimp account. If you don't have an account, use your email program and word processor to develop a newsletter. Then send it out to announce your new book.

Other completed marketing tasks will help you write the newsletter. Include the image file of the book's front cover and use the book blurb as a way to introduce the book.

The newsletter is a great place to also use your short synopsis. If you have received an early review or two, add a few lines from the reviews into the newsletter.

Of vital importance, list the places where a reader can buy the book. Show the links to the major book sellers such as Amazon and Barnes & Noble. Make sure you test the links before you send out the message. A defective link is a complete turnoff to potential buyers.

Press Release

There are a number of sites that will issue your press release. Do a web search to locate a few. Some of them are free. Some charge a modest fee and some are expensive. Generally, the more you pay, the bigger and more prestigious the media outlets contacted.

The purpose of the press release is to tell media sites about the availability of your book. The press release service will distribute the announcement to a large number of media companies.

The press releases sites will have a template or instructions you can use to compose the release.

Press releases start with a short, attention-grabbing headline followed by a longer, but still short, blurb. After that comes the main text area where you can describe your book in depth. This is another place where the short synopsis is useful. Your book cover image also goes into the release as does a short bio and buy links. If you have a trailer, include the link to it.

Once the release has gone out, get a copy and send it to your local media outlets. You may get a write-up, and that will help your marketing efforts.

Web Announcements

Write a blog post announcing the launch of the book. You can use your press release as a template for this post. Make sure you include buy links in the post.

Announce the news with more posts on Facebook, LinkedIn, Goodreads and all your other social media sites. This is big news, but no one knows about it. You have to tell people about it.

Tweet about the event. Use your book blurb (or the first sentence from it) and the cover image to make an interesting tweet along with at least one buy link. Do this multiple times because tweets don't last very long. Within minutes of publication, they will be pushed down so far into the feed they'll rarely be seen. You have to refresh the tweet to keep it current. Each time you reissue it make some minor change so it isn't identical with previous ones.

Email Announcement: This is different from the newsletter you sent out. That one went to readers and fans. This one goes to friends, relatives and acquaintances. Tell them about the availability of your book. Make sure you add a link to the book's webpage and buyer sites. Use your signature file in the message.

In the email, ask the recipients to pass on the email to their own contacts. After all, what's the point of having friends and family if they can't help you pimp your book?

Blog Tour Sites

If you have commissioned a blog tour, it should start running around the launch date. If it's a two-week tour, you probably scheduled it to run one week before and one week after the launch date.

By now, you'll have the schedule of stops and a link to each blog site. Visit each site on the day it talks about your book. In the comment section, post a thank you note. Some sites have followers who start conversations on the topic of the day. If you come across this, participate. Respond to questions. Ask your own questions. Ask if anyone would like a review copy of the ebook. If you get a positive response, you'll need to get an email address to send the ebook along.

If one or more of the sites look like they specialize in your genre, you may want to visit that site occasionally and post comments. This will make it easier for you to use the site for future promotions.

Keep the list of blog site links. It is valuable information. Possibly, for your next book you can set up your own blog tour using these stops, or you can ask the bloggers if they'd like to review the new book. They may also be receptive to a guest post from you about the new book.

Booklife

Booklife is part of Publisher's Weekly but it's dedicated to self-published authors and books. https://booklife.com.

It offers an array of services that you can take advantage of. Some are free and some cost money.

After you start an account, you can place your book, the cover image, the blurb and other material on its website. Spread the link far and wide.

You can submit your book for a free review, but the site only reviews a small portion of the requests it receives. It's free, so why not go for it? If your book is reviewed, it will get publicity on a widely viewed site

If you click on the services icon, you will go to a list of services such as editing, web design and others. Booklife doesn't offer these services itself; instead it lists people and companies who do provide the services.

Booklife offers an advertising program that gives the book widespread attention. The book will appear in a copy of Publishers Weekly and will be promoted on the Booklife site and on its Facebook and Twitter accounts. The promotion costs $149.

Booklife also offers two contests. One is for fiction and the other for non-fiction. They are run at different times of the year. The entry fee is $99. In return, your entry is reviewed and an analysis is provided that is quite detailed. It assesses your submission in the following categories:

- Plot/Idea
- Originality
- Prose
- Character/Execution
- Overall

And of course, you have a chance to win a prize.

Chapter 8: Post-launch

Overview

From this point forward, it's just marketing unless you decide to publish a new version of your book, such as an audio book.

Here is what this chapter will cover.

Publishing tasks:

- Audio Books

Marketing tasks:

- Write another book
- Get more book reviews
- Increase your social media presence
- Initiate book campaigns
- Organize book giveaways
- Sell physical books

Let's move on!

Publishing tasks

Audio Books

Creating an audio book is quite a different experience from writing a book. It's a task that can't occur until after the book is written because a voice-over artist (or the author) reads the completed book into a recording device.

Without going into much detail, this is how the process goes.

While it is possible for the author to do the reading, it may not be the best alternative for two reasons. To make a quality recording requires expensive recording equipment, and an author probably doesn't have the voice training to produce a recording that will hold a listener's attention.

Assuming you don't go the DIY route, you'll need an audio book producer. One such company is ACX, a large audio book producer that is past of the Amazon universe. You will also need another ISBN and a revised cover.

You'll have to start an account at https://www.acx.com. The first step in getting your book converted is to upload a sample text. This will be perused by voice-over artists, and if they are interested in your book, they will make a recording of the sample text, and these recordings will be sent to you. If you get a few sample recordings, you can choose which artist you want to work with. The next step is to negotiate the artist's payment for the book recording and voice-over artists don't come cheap. Once that is finished, you send the artist the complete text, descriptions of the characters and any special instructions on how you want the main characters to sound.

After the artist records the book, it is your job to read your book while simultaneously listening to the recording. If you detect any errors, you'll have to note the exact spot in the recording where the error occurred. When you're finished, you send the artist a list of errors and the artist corrects the recording and sends you a new master recording for you to listen to and approve.

The actual process is more involved that what my brief overview described.

In summary, commissioning an audio book is a complicated and time consuming endeavor, and listening to the recorded version of your book is a weird experience for the author.

Marketing Tasks

Write Another Book

It may surprise you to learn that many surveys and studies show that one of the best marketing tools for your new book is to write another book. Why? Look at your Amazon Central page or your Goodreads Author page. They show only a single book. That's not very impressive. Readers will think you're a one-shot author and not worthy of their consideration. The reason for this is that readers tend to follow authors they like. Oftentimes, they'll read a book, like it and immediately read another book by the same author. Having a second and a third book on the pages will attract these readers and add luster to your name and catalog.

The more books you have, the more impressive your Amazon Central page and your Goodreads Author page will look. The same goes for your author page on Barnes & Noble and other sites.

If your first book is a novel, write another one. If you use the same main characters in the second book, you have a series and that's good. Many readers will read all the books in a series.

If your book is non-fiction, your choices may be more limited. If your first book is about home surgery, perhaps you can expand it into a series with a book about doing kidney transplants on the kitchen table. Expand the series even further with a third book: one that covers appendicitis removals.

Whatever your second book is about, it's time to get started on writing it. Make sure you blog about the new book and give folks an estimate of when to expect it. Update the blog to report on your progress. These posts don't have to be long. The purpose is to get people familiar with your new project and to get them to remember the book's name.

By the way, the process for the second book will be much simpler than for the first book. In the publishing process, you now have a cover artist and an editor. For marketing, you have websites and social media accounts. If you're satisfied with the packagers used on the first book, that is another task you won't have to work on.

Get More Book Reviews

I don't believe there is such a thing as "enough" reviews. One of your post-launch chores is to continue to look for sources of new reviews.

I have heard (but haven't experienced) that Amazon helps you advertise your book if the book gets 50 or more reviews. Trust me, that ain't easy to do, but it is a great goal to have.

There are several strategies you can use to acquire more reviews.

Goodreads groups are a fertile area to request reviews. Use these groups as your first recourse. A few such groups are listed in the next topic in this chapter.

Another approach is to contact a review site. There are a number of these on the web. A simple search will give you a list of sites offering to get book reviews in return for a price. Let me be clear: if you use one of these services, you are *not* buying a review. You're paying for a review *service* that will put your book in front of many potential reviewers who may or may not elect to review your book. Reviewers who chose to read your book are not paid by the review service. What you are paying for when you sign up for a review service is access to all the potential reviewers on its list.

Some of the review services will not deliver the goods. They talk a good story about the many reviewers they have on their list, but you won't get the number of reviews you signed up for. Some sites simply don't have enough readers on their list to deliver the reviews. Others, a small number, are just scammers looking to rip off authors.

Another strategy is to give away copies of your book. More on that topic later in this chapter.

Still another method is to use your social media contacts. Ask if anyone wants a free ebook review copy. I've found this tactic to be marginally effective. The main reason is that some people ask for a review copy only because it's free. They have no intention of ever writing a review. Some readers won't like the book and won't write a negative review. My experience is that between 25% to 50% of these readers will write a review. However, ebooks don't cost you anything to send to potential reviewers so you aren't incurring any costs.

Some readers might be reluctant to write a review because they aren't sure how to go about doing it. You can help them out by sending along a review form that will assist those people in putting together a review. I have a fiction and a non-fiction review form in Chapter 10: Additional Resources. Attach the appropriate form to email requests. It can't hurt.

There are reputable sites you can use to get prestigious reviews, such as Kirkus Reviews. You can find it here: Kirkusreviews.com. This is a site that will review your book, but it requires a large fee ($425 at this writing). Once you pay, you will get a review and you'll see it before it's published. You can then decide if you want it to go public or not. This prevents a stinker of a review from seeing the light of day. If you agree to let it go public, the review will appear on the website and will attract attention. A Kirkus review also looks great on Amazon and other seller websites. Since you paid for it, Amazon does not allow the review to be posted against your book like all the other reviews. However, you can add it to the book on your Amazon Central page under "editorial reviews."

Increase Your Social Media Presence

With your book now available, it's time to increase your social media contacts. One effective way to do this is to become active in groups dedicated to writing and reading. Facebook, LinkedIn and Goodreads all have such groups. You can also explore other social media sites such as Pinterest, Reddit, Instagram and others. Join them if they seem right for you.

Here are a few groups you can join on Goodreads:
- Indie and Self-published Author Support: https://www.goodreads.com/group/show/154447-support-for-indie-authors
- Authors and Reviewers: https://www.goodreads.com/group/show/103713-authors-reviewers
- Support for Indie Authors: https://www.goodreads.com/group/show/103713-authors-reviewers
- Advanced Copies for Review and Book Giveaways: https://www.goodreads.com/group/show/58575-advanced-copies-for-review-book-giveaways

With LinkedIn, potential groups to join include:
- New Authors Need Marketing Ideas: https://www.linkedin.com/groups/1725677/

- Book Marketing Tips: https://www.linkedin.com/groups/1848415/
- Self-published and Indie Authors Networking Group: https://www.linkedin.com/groups/2826012/
- Book Story: https://www.linkedin.com/groups/5148410/

Facebook also has a number of groups for authors. My experience with those groups is they tend to be an endless array of 'buy my book' posts and I dropped out of them. There may be more suitable groups to search for. How you go about increasing your web presence is a personal choice. However, I can offer a few words of advice.

Don't start arguments. You won't win them, not on the web anyway. All you'll do is annoy some of your contacts. And I would advise you to ignore arguments others have started, even if you have an opinion and an urge to jump in. On the other hand, don't be too bland. A little controversy can go a long way.

What you want to do in the groups is reply to questions and to join discussions on topics you feel you're qualified to talk about.

Don't pimp your book in the groups, even if others are doing exactly that. Reserve book marketing tweets and posts for non-group activities.

Initiate Book Promotions

If you budgeted for book promotions, now is the time to start one. But first you have to make a decision: how much are you willing to spend on a promotion? This is somewhat of a loaded question because promotions come in a number of flavors: inexpensive, moderately expensive and very expensive.

This task will require research on your part. I can provide some explanations and leads, but you will have to dig into the guts of other websites to find out all you can before committing money.

Some promotional sites are easy to understand and easy to use. Some, like Google Ads, are filled with techno-babble and are difficult to follow.

Generally, the more you spend the bigger your reach (i.e the more potential readers you'll reach), but this isn't a hard and fast rule.

Promotional websites pop up continuously, and a web search will give you a list of sites to check on. Here is a link to a webpage that lists a hundred or more book promotion sites: https://www.readersintheknow.com/list-of-book-promotion-sites. The list contains a few sites that no longer exist, and I'm not recommending any sites in the list. Perform your due diligence in going through the list. Some of the sites will only promote free books. As a former sales manager, I don't understand the logic behind spending money to give away books. Other sites will only promote books that are available on Kindle.

Then there are promotional sites which are nothing but scams. It is in your best interest to read *all* the fine print before you commit money to a promotional site that looks suspicious. What does suspicious mean? For starters, if a site *guarantees* a certain number of book sales, it most certainly is suspicious. This is because, given the total flakiness of readers, no one can guarantee a level of sales. Before you commit money to any promotion site that hasn't been recommended to you, ask about it on your LinkedIn and Goodreads groups.

Costs

There are several different types of promotions. In one, you pay a flat fee to promote your book. With these, you fill in a data sheet with the title, author, description, price, buy links and the cover. The site sends out the information in an email or newsletter and (hopefully) people buy a copy of the book.

Most types of promotions are more complicated. First, you have to construct the ad. This usually consists of the book cover or the title and a very short sentence followed by a call-to-action (i.e. Buy Now!) and a link to a site selling your book.

The cost of the ad is a variable. In one version, you pay per thousand impressions. An impression is your ad showing up on some website. You hope the ad results in viewers clicking on it. When they do, they are taken to a page selling your book. Typical prices are a dollar or two per thousand impressions and are usually fixed by the promotional site.

In a second version, you pay a fee every time someone clicks on your ad but you aren't charged by the number of impressions. In these ads, the cost may be twenty-five or fifty cents per click. The fee can also be higher or lower. In most case, you set the price you want to pay.

With either version, you construct the ad using a set of options. You can set a start and end date, a daily budget and a total budget. Depending on the length of the ad and the daily budget, these promotions can become expensive, so you have to monitor your spending closely. Google Ads (formerly Adwords) is typical of this type of promotional site. The success of these ad campaigns hinges on the keywords you select for the ad. Google has tools to help you select the correct ones.

The third — very expensive — kind of promotion involves hiring a promotion company to promote your book. These promotions will require you to sign a contract and pay up front. In return, the company will do an enormous amount of work promoting your book. Since there are large amounts of money involved here, make sure you do a lot of research before signing up with such a company. LinkedIn may be a good place to start your research.

Promo Sites

I've run a lot of book ads and here are some of the sites I've used or looked into. The following is not a set of recommendations.

Fussy Librarian: https://www.thefussylibrarian.com is an inexpensive site. How much your ad costs depends upon the genre. I've used this site a number of times with mixed results.

Bookbub: https://www.bookbub.com/launch is a big site that has two types of promotions: very expensive email lists and pay per click. Their email lists are extensive and Bookbub is very selective about whom they allow to advertise, even if you're willing to pay the fee. You can submit your book free of charge and you'll be informed if it's selected or not. If your book is selected, you pay the fee (Think a minimum of $800 or $900 dollars: it keeps going up!) The higher the price of your book during the promotion, the greater the fee. If selected, you will sell a lot of books. Will it cover the cost of the campaign? I don't know. I've used Bookbub several times in the past, but that was when it first started out and the fee was a hundred bucks or so. The site became wildly successful, and the prices shot through the roof and it became very tough to get selected.

Bookbub also has pay per click campaigns you can use. They work similar to Google Ads.

If your book is on Amazon, you can use its Amazon Marketing Services https://advertising.amazon.com. Amazon has several options available including pay per click and other types of ad campaigns.

When it comes to promotional companies, they are the very expensive ones mentioned earlier. I'm familiar with two of them: Smith Publicity and Author Marketing Expert

Smith Publicity https://www.smithpublicity.com is an international publicity company.

Author Marketing Expert https://www.amarketingexpert.com is run by Penny Sansevieri, who is considered a social media marketing guru.

In conclusion

Book promotions can be used to spread the word about your book and even sell copies. The promotions can also drain your wallet. Don't sign up with a promotional site without researching it. Once the promotion is running, monitor the results and especially your spending.

Organize Book Giveaways

One way to gain readers is to give away copies of your book. Giveaways are different from running an ad promoting a book that is free. Giveaways are much more targeted.

There are a number of reasons to run a giveaway. Firstly, some of these readers may post a review. Secondly, the giveaway may enable you to grow your list of emails. Thirdly, it increases your name recognition. Finally, it can lead to future sales.

If you give away a print book, you'll incur both production and postage costs in getting the books from the packager, and then you'll have more postage costs when you send it out. If you give away an ebook, it doesn't cost you anything. Ebooks don't have production costs and they don't have postage requirements. However, print book giveaways will attract more interest; especially if you sign the book with the reader's name.

Here are a few ways you can give away the book.

- You can write a blog post stating that you're giving away X copies of your new book in a random drawing to people who sign up via an email form. You can use Mailchimp for this effort. Mailchimp has a simple email signup form you can, use and you'll get a notice every time someone fills out the form. At the end of the signup period, select the winners and attach the ebook to an email. Ask the winners to write a review if they enjoy the book. Spread the word about your giveaway on Twitter, Facebook, LinkedIn and wherever else you have accounts.

- You can commission an online raffle using a site like Rafflecopter: https://www.rafflecopter.com. This site has a paid monthly subscription plan. Sign up for it if you plan to run a lot of raffles, otherwise use its free trial offer. Use your social media accounts to promote the raffle.
- If you have your book on Smashwords, you can change the price of the book to a free download and run this sale for a limited period of time. Promote the freebie using social media.
- If you have your book on Kindle and it's enrolled it in Kindle Select you can offer your book for free five days in every quarter. Promote the offer using social media.

The disadvantage of using Smashwords and Kindle as the way to give away your book is you don't know who downloaded it. In this case, your chances of gaining reviews are next to nothing. A reason for this is the capacity of ereaders. It is virtually unlimited. Readers can (and many do) download every interesting free book they come across. They may read your book some day, but that day can be far into the future. In other words, the benefits of your book giveaway are marginal at best.

Another tactic many authors use is to permanently list their book as a free download. I don't believe this action has any benefits. An author should want to *sell* his book, not give it away forever. Running an occasional giveaway has some benefits to the author. Offering a permanent free download has few, if any, of those benefits.

Physical Book Selling

Ebooks are sold almost exclusively on the internet. Print books are sold via the web, in bookstores and at events you attend. Libraries are another potential market.

Book stores

Book stores are a tough nut to crack for self-published authors, especially if it's a first book and the author has no name recognition. Most book stores in this country use Ingram as their distributor. If your book is distributed by Ingram, is returnable and has the industry standard discount (55%) there is a chance book stores will order your book and put it on their shelves for a while. However, book stores will not know about the book's existence unless you tell them about it. Contacting book stores one at a time is a mind-numbing activity, especially if you pursue out-of-area and out-of-state book stores. The only cost-effective way to query these stores is by using email.

Just because your book isn't on a shelf in a book store doesn't mean the store can't order a copy if a customer requests one. Barnes & Noble and other book stores can order a print copy of the book just by entering the ISBN number or the book title into their computer system. Within a few days, the book will arrive ready to be picked up by the customer who ordered it.

If your print book packager is Kindle, there is no, nada, zippo, zilch, not-a-prayer of the book store ordering a copy of the book to put on its shelves. Kindle will not allow returns, and that is a deal breaker as far as the book store is concerned. Although the book store won't put the Kindle book on its shelves, it can and will order a copy if a customer requests it.

Assuming you get books into a book store, does that mean the store will arrange a book signing for you? Probably not. If you're an unknown author, the book store owner may feel he is wasting his time because few people will come in to see and hear an author they never heard of.

Libraries

Most libraries rely primarily on Baker & Taylor as their distributor, but they will also use Ingram. If your book isn't distributed by one of these two companies, you have very little chance of getting the book onto library shelves unless you give them a free copy.

Once you get the book into a library (start with your local ones), ask if they will arrange a book reading and signing. A library may be more receptive to the signing than a book store will be. They'll usually put a blurb into the local paper, thus increasing your exposure. Make sure you have a supply of books to sell. This is should be a budget item that you fund if you have a print edition of your book.

Some libraries may want a slice of revenue if they allow you to sell books at the reading. My experience is they'll want ten percent of whatever you make. I think it's a great deal. Libraries need all the financial help they can get.

Consignments

Consignment selling means the book store will take copies of the book, but the store will not order them. They will only accept copies of the book that you order and pay for. This relieves the book store from initially paying for the books and handling returns later on. In other words, it improves their cashflow and transfers inventory management to the author.

Under consignment deals, the book store will keep a percentage of all book sales and the author gets what's left. Typically, the book store will want 25% to 40% of the sale revenue.

A consignment deal typically will last three to six months. At the end of the period, you settle the payment issue and walk away with the unsold books under your arm and a check in your pocket. If some books were sold, the book store may agree to renew the deal.

Consignment selling requires a contract that is signed by the author and the store. The contract will contain the book title, number of books in the deal, the book price and the store's percentage of sales.

You can find blank contracts at a number of websites including Legalzoom: https://www.legalzoom.com and Rocketlawyer: https://

www.rocketlawyer.com.

There is one thing to keep in mind with consignment deals: ask whether your book will be displayed on a shelf or dumped in the storage room where no one will ever see them. If your books are slated to go into storage, you may want to rethink the consignment deal.

Book Events

Book events are gatherings such as book fairs where readers go to peruse tables staffed by authors and loaded with their books. These are usually run by libraries, at least around where I live. Of course, these are difficult to get involved with if you only have ebooks. One way around this obstacle is to take your ebook and burn it onto CDs. Make sure you get a label program to dress up the CD so it doesn't look like you're selling pirated material. You can also use small thumbnail drives for this activity, but they will cost more than burning CDs.

Other book events are street fairs and flea markets. In these you may have to rent a table from the event's organizers. That means for you to make a profit on the event, you first have to sell enough books to cover the cost of the table.

Print Book Ads

A way for a self-published author to alert book stores about the book is to use an ad in industry magazines. One such magazine is Publishers Weekly. https://www.publishersweekly.com.

PW has a monthly section that lists self-published books. Each book listing shows the cover, a short blurb, the ISBN and the retail price.

The ads are a bit pricey, however: $149 per book per issue.

Chapter 9: Your Book Company

Overview

Now that your book is launched, let's switch subjects and talk about the business of being an author because there are business issues to talk about.

Here's a list of topics in this chapter:
- Your book company (yeah, you read that one correctly!)
- Taxes
- Revenue splits
- Break even analysis

Some of the material in this chapter may have been covered briefly earlier in the book. I think the issues are important enough to discuss them again here.

Much of the material in this chapter is taken from my book *Business Basics for Authors*.

Let's get started.

Your Book Company

Once you decide to publish a book, you suddenly become the owner of a company. The purpose of the company is to market and sell your book. Whether the book is put out by a publisher or you self-published it, the marketing responsibility belongs to your new company. Here is an organizational chart for your new company.

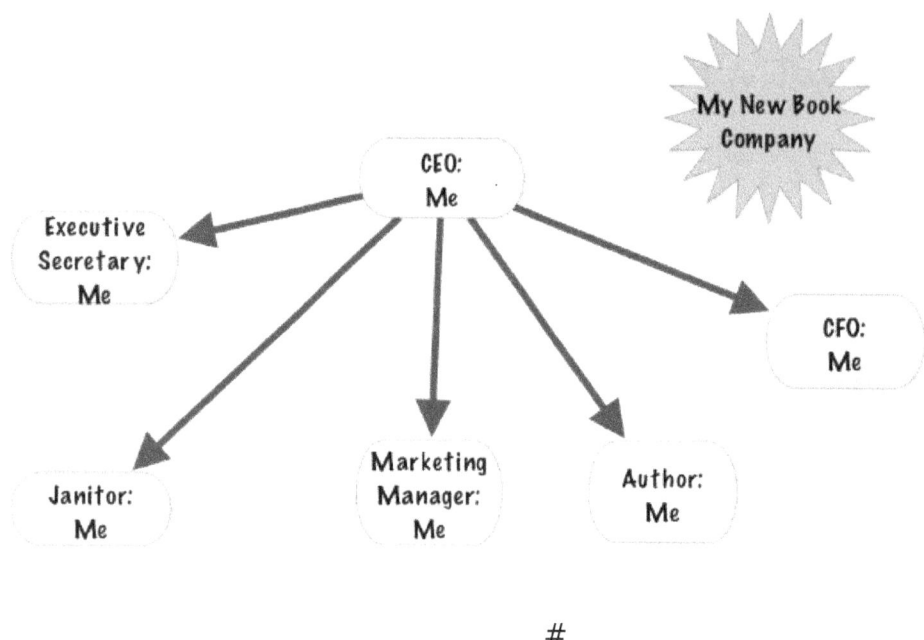

#

If you're puzzled about how this company came about, it started when you developed the strategic plan for your book. Every company uses a strategic plan. From this plan, you developed your tactical plans. As you complete the marketing tasks in this book, you are implementing the tactics in your strategic plan. In other words, you have been working as the CEO even though you hadn't realized you were doing it.

Since you are now the CEO of a company, it behooves you to understand some business fundamentals. And why do authors need to know this? In the course of marketing your book you will incur expenses, and by selling the book you will receive income. If your income exceeds your expenses, you will have earned a profit. The terms 'income' and 'profit' also relate to tax issues.

There is one big takeaway from this idea of owning a company: you have to make business decisions, not ego-driven decisions. A good example of this principle is in establishing the book price. You, as the author, may think your book is worthy of a premium price, but you, as the CEO, must decide that the book price will be in line with similar self-published books.

You will face more decisions of this ilk in your new career as a CEO. Make sure you suppress your author ego when making them.

Taxes

Revenue from the sale of your book and the expenses incurred during the course of business are reported on Schedule C Profit or Loss from Business. This form is for use in the United States. If you live in a different country, you'll have to do some research to find the proper form. You can file the Schedule C without doing anything special or unique and without even mentioning your company name, if you have one.

You can apply for a separate tax id number for your company if you want. To do so, you must fill out Form SS-4, Application for Employer Identification Number (EIN) and submit it to the IRS. There are blanks on the form to enter your company name, but that is optional. You can get an EIN form at this website: https://www.irs.gov/businesses/small-businesses-self-employed/employer-id-numbers. The form is free from the IRS, but other websites will charge for a copy of the form.

After you send in the SS-4 form, eventually you'll get a response with your unique tax ID number. It looks different from your social security number, which is also a tax ID number.

Why bother with this tax ID nonsense? Having a tax ID and a company name grants you some legitimacy with the Internal Revenue Service. If the IRS determines that your writing is really a hobby and not a business, it will limit how much of your expenses you can deduct. Having the tax ID with a company name will help convince the IRS that you're a serious writer/author and that you are indeed a legitimate business.

Before you complete the EIN request, you'll have to make a decision about what type of company you have. The simplest choices come down to a Sole Proprietorship or an LLC, a Limited Liability Company.

Sole Proprietorship: these companies are relatively simple, or as simple as anything relating to taxes can be. The owner of the sole proprietorship is in complete control of every aspect of the business, including the sale or transfer of the assets and even selling off the company itself. Another advantage is that there are no corporate taxes to pay. There may be some legal issues on the state level, so check your state's website for information on Sole Proprietorships. On the negative side of sole proprietorships, the owner is legally liable for the debts and obligations of the company. Any capital required to operate the business comes from the owner.

Limited Liability Company: these entities are more complex then the sole proprietorship. It combines some of the advantages of the sole proprietorship with some of the advantages of a corporation. One such advantage is the owner of the LLC has the same level of personal protection from debts as a corporation enjoys. Another is that the LLC will not pay taxes the way corporations do. The LLC owners are responsible for the taxes and pay them on their personal tax forms.

A disadvantage is that the legal requirements to set up an LLC vary by state and you may need to get a lawyer involved.

Revenue Splits

Let's talk about what happens when books get sold through your packagers. You'll get some of the money, some of the money will go to the packagers, and some will go to the distributors. How much does each get? Here is how three packagers split up the sales revenue.

Let's assume your ebook sells for $3.99 and the print book for $14.99.

Smashwords: With this packager, the revenue split is simple. If you sell an ebook through the Smashwords site, the split is 70/30 with you getting the 70% share. So for each ebook sold on the site, you'll get $2.80. If the book is sold through a site Smashwords distributes to, such as the iStore or B&N, the split is 60/40 and you make $2.40 on each book.

On the Smashwords site, you'll find pie charts that show exactly how much you'll make in each case and for whatever price you establish.

Kindle Ebooks: Here the ebook split becomes a bit more complicated because Kindle uses two revenue sharing plans. One plan calls for a 35/65 split and the other 70/30. The 70/30 split is not available if your book is priced at less than $2.99. If there are any advantages in keeping the 35/65 split for a book that is eligible for the 70/30 plan, I don't know what that advantage is. With your $3.99 book, you won't get exactly 70% because Kindle levies a delivery fee (???) on the book sale and the size of the fee increases for bigger books. If your book has graphics in it, the download fee will increase dramatically. As with Smashwords, you'll get $2.80 for each book sold at the US Amazon site with the 70% split minus delivery fees, of course.

Kindle doesn't use distributors the way Smashwords does. Kindle won't place your book with other web sellers such as the Kobo site, but it will put the book on non-USA Amazon sites. This is an option you have to select. Some of these sites have only the 35% option available unless you enroll your book in Kindle Select and make it unavailable to other packagers and distributors. I don't enroll in the Kindle Select Program. My reason for not using the Kindle Select Program is because I want my books to be available on as many different sites as possible. This is a maxim in Marketing 101 and, in my opinion, the only one who benefits from the Kindle Select Program is Amazon. But feel free to ignore me and enroll if you wish. If you do sign up for Kindle Select, the program will run for three months. It will *automatically renew* unless you find the auto renew option and unselect it. By default, this option is always selected.

With the non-USA sites, how much money you get on a sale is difficult to predict exactly, because the sale is made in a foreign currency and a currency exchange has to be made before you can get paid.

There is a "but" to the seventy percent split option. The seventy percent split only applies to book sales made through an Amazon site by a customer within one of twenty countries (at the time of this writing). These countries include almost all of North America, Europe and parts of Asia. If, for instance, a customer from Honduras or Antigua bought your book through the Amazon USA site, you'd only get thirty-five percent on that sale. Why? Let's just chalk this up as one more inexplicable Amazon fact.

Kindle Print Books: For your print book, there are a number of possible revenue splits. If your book is sold through the USA Amazon site, the split is 40/60 and you'll get $6.00 on each book. Kindle will distribute your paperback to Barnes & Noble and, if sold there, your cut will be less than $6.00.

Kindle will distribute your book to the European Amazon sites if you let it. And why wouldn't you? For books sold in non-USA sites the exchange rate comes up again, and any revenue figure I quote will change with the currency exchange rate. In a nutshell, your cut will be around $6.00, but it will be higher or lower depending upon you know what.

Other packagers will have their own revenue split methods. Make sure you understand them and ask questions if their explanation is a bit fuzzy or obscure.

Break Even Analysis

Break even analysis is a tool that allows you to understand the risks involved in funding a project or a marketing campaign. Marketing campaigns can be used to achieve two important goals. One is extending your name recognition. The second is to increase sales. Trailers can be used for the first goal. I doubt a trailer will directly sell many books, but it can make readers acquainted with your book and that is a good thing. Initiating a marketing campaign frequently, but not always, involves money. These expenditures should be viewed as an investment and as such should be expected to bring in a return on the investment. That's fancy business talk meaning you should get back the money you spent and then some. Before spending the upfront money for the marketing campaign, do a break even analysis to see if you have a snowball's chance to recover your investment. There is an easy way to do this using spreadsheet templates. The templates are already configured and all you have to do is plug in the variable numbers.

As an example, let's say you come across this attractive marketing site. Here's the deal: for an upfront price of $150, the site will advertise your book for two weeks, but the book price must be reduced to half-price or less. To simplify the first example, we'll restrict sales to your Smashwords packager with its seventy percent royalty. Your book normally sells for $3.99 and you want to see break even points for prices of $1.99 (50% discount) and $1.49 (63% discount).

The Numbers spreadsheet program (for Mac computers) comes with a break even template. MS Excel also has a similar pre-built spreadsheet. Here is a link to a site where you download an Excel template: https://templates.office.com/?legRedir=true&CorrelationId=fe77895d-b097-4c11-805c-8d8aa79ba731

The Numbers spreadsheet has an item called Variable Cost per Unit that has to be factored in. This is frequently called Cost of Sales. In the case of

How to Self-publish and Market a Book 124

your book, this is the amount of the sale Smashwords collects from each book sale. With the $1.99 price option, the cost of sales is $.60 per book and for the $1.49 price option, it's $.45.

If you run the analysis, it shows that with the $1.99 price option and a fixed cost of $150 (the cost of the marketing campaign) you have to sell 108 copies of the book to break even. Every book sale over 108 will produce a profit for you on this ad campaign. For instance, if you sell 160 copies, your revenue will be $318 dollars with a cost of $246 netting a profit of $72. This spread sheet analysis is pasted here. You can see the components and the graph showing costs and sales. The numbers in the yellow section are the variables you have to enter for your study.

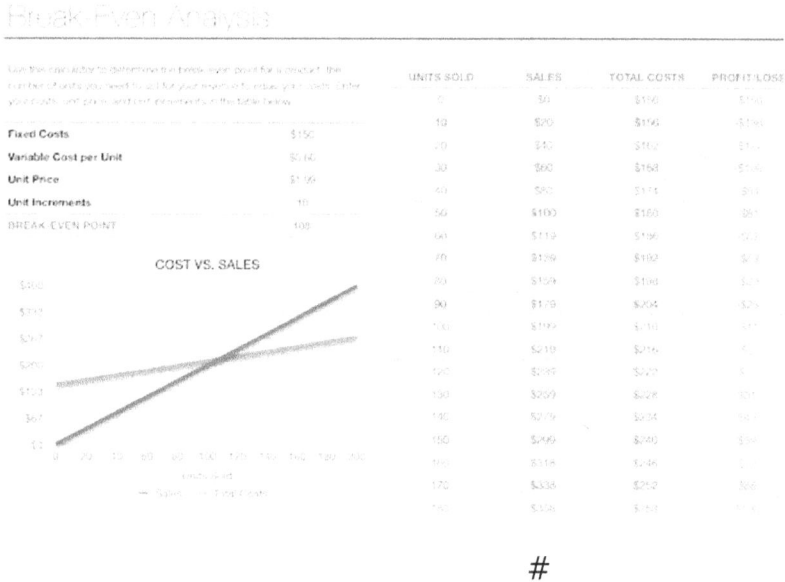

\#

The beauty of a spreadsheet like this is that it is simple to run another analysis for the $1.49 option. Adjusting the data for the new study yields these results. You have to sell 144 books to recover the $150 upfront charge. If you manage to sell 200 copies, the results are: $298 in book sales and $240 in costs leaving a profit of $58.

After you run the break even analyses, you're left to answer this question: Can I sell 108 (or 144) copies of my book? Much of the answer depends on the site that provides the marketing campaign. If it has enough clout to reach a large number of potential book buyers then the answer is: yes, you may reach the break even point and beyond. On the other hand, if the site is obscure with no real clout, then the answer is: no, you'll probably lose your shirt on this deal.

This promotion using a Kindle ebook would be different from the Smashwords promotion. This is because the seventy percent royalty option with Kindle only applies to books whose price is $2.99 or more. Below the $2.99 price, the royalty is thirty-five percent. This makes the Variable Cost per Unit for the $1.99 option $1.29. For the $1.49 option, this figure is $.99.

Running the break even analysis for a Kindle promotion yields these results. For the $1.99 option, you have to sell 214 books to break even. For the $1.49 option, the break even point is 300 books.

The spreadsheet for the $1.99 option is shown below. Keep in mind, this analysis ignores the Kindle download fee.

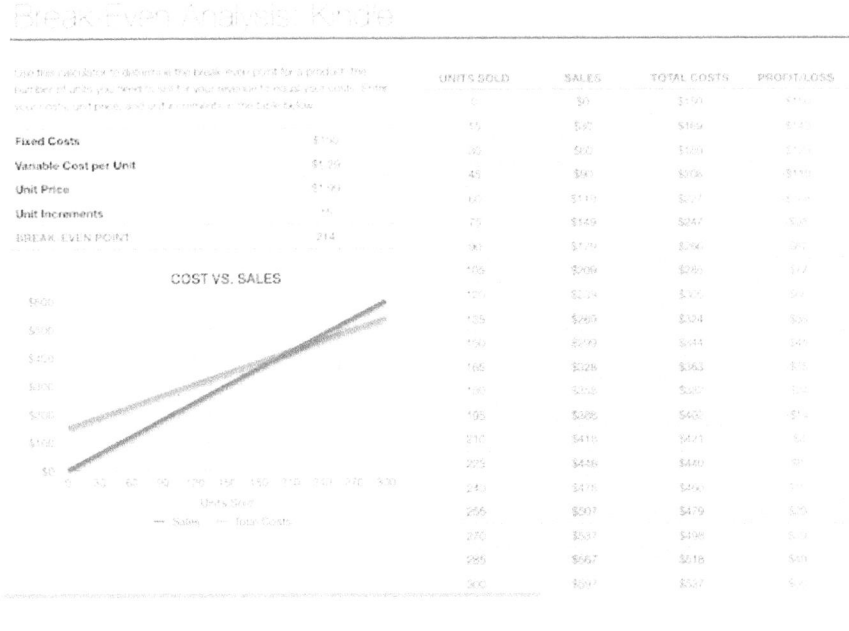

#

This type of analysis has implications. In many cases, the company running the promotion is making big bucks while you are struggling to break even. In the example above, you are paying the promotion site $150 to send out emails to its client list and to put your book prominently on its website. There is no guarantee as to how many books you'll sell, and no matter how many or how few you sell, it still costs you $150. Nevertheless, this can be a good way to get your book into the hands of many readers who otherwise would have never heard of you or your book.

This example demonstrates that like almost everything in marketing, it's fraught with financial peril.

Chapter 10: Additional Resources

Overview

This chapter contains resources you can use on your self-publishing and marketing project. Most of this information, while important, doesn't fit neatly into any of the other chapters so it got dumped here.

Here is a list of topics in this chapter

- Marketing task prioritization
- Support information web page
- Checklist
- SWOT Analysis
- Scams
- Marketing help
- Business help
- Fiction book review questionnaire
- Non-fiction book review questionnaire
- Trailer creation
- My marketing plan
- Complete index of tasks

Marketing Task Prioritization

What if you can't work on all the marketing tasks listed in this book? After all, life has a way of butting into one's writing and publishing work.

Obviously, not all marketing tasks are created equal, so the question comes down to this: What marketing tasks are the most important?

Here is my answer to that question. If you have limited time to spend on marketing, make sure you do the following:

- Create a strategic marketing plan: Chapter 2
- Get a webpage: Chapter 4
- Develop keywords: Chapter 5
- Write a book blurb: Chapter 5
- Join Goodreads: Chapter 3
- Ask for Goodreads book review requests: Chapter 6
- Write a short synopsis: Chapter 5

On the other hand, what marketing tasks are the least important?

- Get a trailer: Chapter 6
- Do a blog tour: Chapter 7

Support Web Page

I've put together a support web page for this book. It has a lot of material on it including a number of pdf files that can be downloaded (free of charge) and videos you can watch. The location is: https://padlet.com/hanque/b0boum9fw405.

One of the graphics on the site is a graphical mind-map of the Table of Contents. I used that mind-map extensively in the layout of this book (I love mind-maps!). It may not be useful to you, but I couldn't resist showing off a bit. It is the third one I constructed for the book (the first two were much different and I rejected them). I completed the final one before I started writing the book, and it still took a lot of shuffling around before I hit on the final version.

For the record, I used MindNode 5 software https://mindnode.com to develop the Table of Contents mind-map.

Checklist

Keeping track of a complicated project such as self-publishing and marketing a book is a tough job. It's easy to get lost in the details and it's sometimes difficult to remember what is done and what isn't.

To address this problem, I built a checklist. Pasted below is a graphic showing part of it. It's a rather large spreadsheet which is why the text is so small.

Task	Function	Status	Time Frame	% Complete	Budget Item?	Cost	Notes
Establish Launch Date	Publishing	Not Started	6 months	0	No	$0	As author, you get to establish the launch date, you can complete all these tasks
Develop Publishing Budget	Publishing	Not Started	6 months	0	No	$0	Covers and professional editing will be in your b
Book Title Search	Publishing	Not Started	6 months	0	No	$0	Results may be surprising
Complete Manuscript	Publishing	Not Started	6 months	0	No	$0	Don't think a first draft satisfies this item
Recruit Beta Readers	Publishing	Not Started	6 months	0	No	$0	These fellow writers have the important job of p
Send Manuscript to Beta Readers	Publishing	Not Started	6 months	0	No	$0	Ask if they can complete their comments within

#

There are two versions of it, one for Mac users and the other for PC users. The Mac version is interactive with drop-down checkboxes and sliders. Alas, the PC version is static.

In the Mac version (numbers format) of the spreadsheet, the status column is show as "Not Started" for all tasks. This can be changed via a dropdown checkbox to "Underway" or "Completed". Tasks that require funding are clearly shown and there is a space to add the cost so you can track this detail. Furthermore, if a marketing task won't be used, you can change the status to 'Not applicable.'

Each task can be moved up or down if desired, and the timeframe column has a dropdown checkbox that can be changed to reflect the changed timeframe.

While the PC version (xls format) doesn't have the interactive features of the Max version, it is still a very useful tool to track your progress.

The spreadsheet itself can't be inserted into the book, but I'll send you a copy of the checklist if you want one. Send me an email requesting the "Book Launch Checklist" and I'll send you the file as an attachment. Specify whether you want the Mac or the PC version.

Send the request to hanque99 (at) gmail (dot) com.

SWOT Analyses

SWOT stands for Strengths, Weaknesses, Opportunities and Threats. The SWOT analysis is a standard way to identify the problems in a set of circumstances.

Here is the Wikipedia definition: *SWOT analysis is a strategic planning technique used to help a person or organization identify strengths, weaknesses, opportunities, and threats related to business competition or project planning.*

In the situation addressed by this book, SWOT means the state of affairs facing an author who wishes to self-publish and market a book for the first time.

Here is the usual format for a SWOT Chart although it comes in a few different flavors.

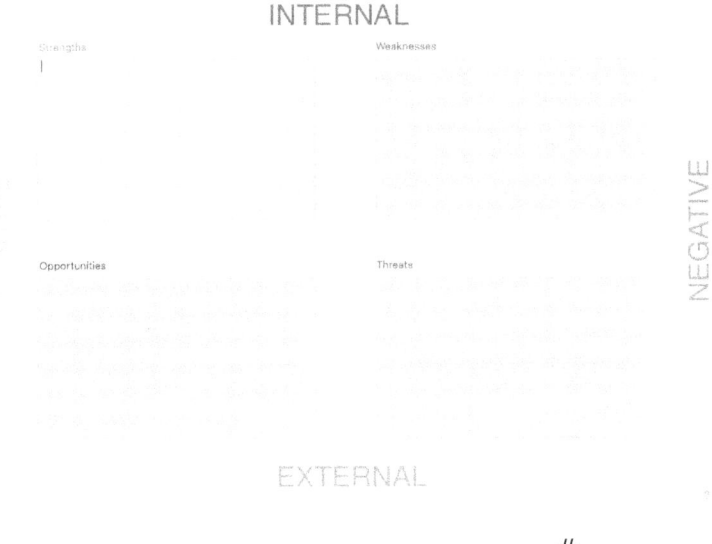

#

As you can see, there are four labels for the chart: internal, external, positive and negative. The colored boxes are where the chart gets its name. The boxes are labeled: strengths, weaknesses, opportunities and threats.

I've put together three SWOT charts, one each for Self-publishing, Book Marketing and Author Business. Rather than clutter up the book with charts which may not be of interest to some, I put them on a support web page along with instructions on how to use them. Each of the three SWOT charts can be individually downloaded. The location of the web page is: https://padlet.com/hanque/b0boum9fw405.

The four colored boxes are explained below.

Strengths: These are your forte. These are things that are within your control.

Weaknesses: These are factors that detract from your strengths. They are issues and problems you have to work on to improve or negate. With time, the weakness may disappear or even become a strength.

Opportunities: These are external factors that can contribute to your success. You may not be able to take advantage of the opportunities because you don't have the time or they require money you can't spend right now. Revisit these occasionally to see if your situation changed and you can work on one or more of them.

Threats: are external factors that you have no control over. You may want to develop a contingency plan to address these issues if they crop up.

Here is a link to an informative article on SWOT plans. https://www.liveplan.com/blog/what-is-a-swot-analysis-and-how-to-do-it-right-with-examples/

So what's the upshot of all this SWOT stuff? If you look at the charts I put on the web page, it boils down to the fact that the job ahead of you is challenging. On the other hand, you have the determination and stamina to write a book. So, why can't you do this self-publishing and marketing stuff? Others have faced this situation and succeeded, so why can't you?

The value of the SWOT charts is to clarify the issues. Once you know what they are, they are easier to address. As unknowns they are impossible to work on.

Despite the apparent negativity displayed by the SWOT charts, y**ou can do this**.

Scams

As an author, especially a newly self-published one, you will be subjected to a barrage of "helpful" offers. Some of the offers will be legitimate and some will be from scam artists. How did all these people find you? Your book is on the internet and so is your name as the book's author. It doesn't take much research for others to find out you're self-published and that this is your first book. Consider this as your initial taste of fame. Once the parties have identified you as a first-time self-publisher, they'll start targeting you with offers to help. Some of them will come by email, others will come via direct messages on social media sites.

Below, I'll discuss a few scams I've come across. These are illustrative examples. There are many more, and new ones pop up all the time because the scammers are very creative.

Be warned. The marketing swamp can be hazardous to your financial health.

Marketing help:

One of the most prevalent scams is an email with a link to an impressive-looking website that describes an incredible way to get your book in front of vast hordes of readers who have been waiting for a book like yours. And they will be willing to help you market your book for only a 'small' consideration.

Be careful when investigating a book marketing service that places ads on other website or sends out emails. Many of these come from scammers who will 'offer' a package of services that will cost an arm and a leg. Check out the service on your LinkedIn and Goodreads groups.

Your account is locked

This is a tacky one. You'll get an email claiming an account you have (like PayPal) has been locked and you need to send your personal information to get it unlocked. One way to uncover this type of scam is to right click or hover the mouse arrow on the email address. If it looks nothing like the site it claims to be from, it's a genuine scam. Delete it and don't click on any links in the body of the email.

Your domain name will expire shortly.

Your domain name must be renewed annually, which gives rise to this scam operation. This is typically done with snail mail (you have to give your home address when you register a domain name, and domain name registration information is public information). The letter will tell you that your domain name is in danger of being lost if it isn't renewed before it expires.

As a *courtesy* (?), the operator will renew it for you for a small charge of perhaps $50 or $100 per domain name. They'll even offer a reduced price to extend the domain name for several years, payable in advance.

Whatever server you use will tell you when the domain name has to be renewed. My domain names are registered through my server, *A Small Orange* and they advise me in advance when the domain name will expire. Mine are automatically renewed as part of the service provided by ASO and it costs $15 per year per domain name.

Throw these offers in the recycling.

Contests

It's imperative that you read the fine print and the FAQs on each contest website. One time I received an email about a contest I hadn't heard about. In reading the FAQs, I came across a statement that said the judges do not read all entries. They pick and choose which ones to read. Say what? Why would an author enter a contest and pay a fee of perhaps a $100 if there is a good chance the book wouldn't be read. In looking at the lists of winners from the previous contests, I was struck by the number of awards that went to books published by a vanity press house with a very unsavory reputation. To me, the winner's list screamed collusion. My advice is always read everything you can about the contests before committing money.

Email Blasts

This one will offer to tell tens of thousands of people about your book via an email announcement. And it only costs a few hundred dollars, which comes out to pennies per announcement. Such a deal! The thing is, ninety-nine point ninety-nine percent of the emails sent out will never be read by the recipients. Most will be ignored or rerouted to the junk mail folder.

A variation on this involves Twitter, Facebook and other websites. For a small fee, the sender will get you a thousand followers. Unfortunately, the followers will have no interest in you or your book.

Book Seller Websites

I found this site when a friend asked me if I used it to sell books. I don't remember the name of the site, but it probably has gone out of business by now. At the site, you could upload a pdf edition of your book and the cover along with the blurb and other information, and the site would produce a web page for the book and display it. It looked attractive, but keep in mind that sites like this will never be a primary sales channel like Kindle, Barnes & Noble, iStore and the others. This is a secondary channel that may sell a book or two occasionally. I checked the revenue distribution and saw that it was 70/30 like Smashwords and Kindle. So far, so good. I did some more checking and the situation went downhill. Fast. The site distributes your sales money to you only after it accumulates a hundred dollars. So, if your book sells for $2.99, your cut will be $2.09. To reach a hundred dollars in sales you'll have to sell forty-eight copies of the book. Through a secondary channel like this, it will take years to accumulate a hundred dollars. The site meanwhile keeps the sales revenue it has collected from your book. And then I read the clincher: to display a book on the site will cost you a hundred dollars per book per year! The amazing thing to me was the large number of books the site displayed. Apparently, those authors didn't understand simple arithmetic or never bothered to read the conditions posted on the site. Always read all the information posted on sites before you agree to use that site. The information isn't always easy to find. Search the FAQs pages and all the other pages on the site. You never know where an interesting tidbit may be buried deep in the hope readers will stop reading before reaching the information.

Blog Tour Operators

Some clever tour operators don't send out requests to bloggers: they simply use their own blog sites. For instance, if the tour operator offers a ten-stop tour, they'll create ten new blog sites and use them for the tours.

Technically, you are getting the ten stops you signed up for, except no one will visit the sites. This is because these ten blogs don't get any traffic. The only people who ever visit them are the authors who think they are on a grand promotional tour.

Vanity Presses

Vanity presses are out to grab as much of your money as they possibly can. They don't care about you or your book. But don't take my word for it. Here's a link to an informative article about vanity presses and other scams you may run into. https://blog.reedsy.com/scams-and-publishing-companies-to-avoid/.

Here's another exercise for you to do: run a web search using the term 'vanity press.' Make sure you read a few of the myriad of articles that show up in the search results.

Remember

Always be vigilant! It's your money at risk!

Marketing Help

Here are a few sites and books you may find useful.

Websites

Penny Sansevieri: Author Marketing Experts: https://www.amarketingexpert.com

Rachael Thompson: https://rachelintheoc.com

Sandra Beckwith: https://buildbookbuzz.com

Joanna Penn: https://www.thecreativepenn.com

Books

The Secrets to Ebook Publishing Success by Mark Coker

Smashwords Book Marketing Guide by Mark Coker

Red Hot Internet Publicity by Penny Sansevieri

30-Day Marketing Challenge by Rachael Thompson

Business Help

IRS forms: http://www.irs.gov/

Starting a small business guide: https://www.rocketlawyer.com/starting-a-business-guide.rl

SBA business planning tool: sba.gov/business-plan

Stratpad: http://www.stratpad.com

Mind Tools: http://www.mindtools.com/index.html

Book Review Forms

It's my observation that many people don't write reviews for books they enjoy because they aren't sure how to go about writing one. To alleviate this problem I wrote up a book review form to help readers compose a short, simple book review.

There are two forms: one for fiction books and a second for non-fiction. You can copy and paste them into a word processor or you can download them from the support website: https://padlet.com/hanque/b0boum9fw405

Fiction Book Review Questionnaire:

On a scale of 1 to 5 (5 being the highest) how would rate this book?

1) Did you like or dislike the book?

2) Please explain why you answered 2) as you did.

If you liked the book, please answer the following questions:

3) Why did you like the book?

4) What didn't you like about the book?

5) Did the main characters seem real and believable to you?

6) Did you want the book to continue beyond the ending?

Use your answers to these questions to write a few sentences about the book. Hint: don't write a brief synopsis.

Non-fiction Book Review Questionnaire:

How many stars, from 1 to 5 would you give this book? (Five is the highest rating)

1) What did you like about the book? (if anything)

2) What didn't you like about the book? (if anything)

3) Did you get the information the author promised in the book blurb and other promotional material?

4) Did the book contain information you weren't expected or didn't know about?

5) Would you recommend this book to others?

Use your answers to these questions to write a few sentences about the book.

Creating a Trailer

If you use a Mac computer, you have all the software you need to create a trailer. How to use that software is described below. If you have a PC, you can follow the details but you'll have to figure out what software to use. A web search will reveal lists of programs available.

On your Mac, you'll use iMovie and Keynote to develop the trailer. iMovie is a powerful software program that can be used to make a trailer and other video productions. Keynote is a presentation program similar to Powerpoint.

To get started you need to create a series of slides describing your book project. I'll use a novel in my example. Besides the body of the slide (what will show on the screen) use the Presenters Notes to write the script you will record later on. Try to keep the trailer length less than two minutes.

Here is a workable set of Keynote presentation slides you can use to build a simple trailer:

• Slide 1: Show the book cover image in the body and paste your book blurb in the Presenters Notes.

• Slide 2: Create several bullet items about your protagonist. Write about the character's motivation in the notes

• Slide 3: Create several bullet items about the antagonist. Write about the character's motivation in the notes

• Slide 4: List the main plot events: Write about how the two characters engage in conflict.

• Slide 5: List book buyer sites. The trailer can't have active links and you don't have any right now

• Slide 6: Book cover image. Write a call to action. (Buy now! Don't miss this thrilling whatever! Etc.)

Once you complete the Keynote presentation slides, export the slides as images. This will produce a folder with a png (or jpg) file for each slide.

Open iMovie and start a new movie. Now drag the slide images into the middle of the iMovie screen. Next, drag each image into the bottom part of the iMovie screen. Each image you drag down there will be set to show for 4 seconds. That's the default value.

For the next step, you'll record an audio track to go with each image. Highlight the first slide (It should be the book image). The image will also show up in the small viewer on the upper right. Click on the microphone.

You'll get a countdown clock. Record the message. Put some enthusiasm into it. Your audio track will appear under the image on the bottom. You'll notice the audio is much longer than the image. Drag the right side of the image to increase the time the image shows on screen. Make it the same length as the audio clip.

If you put the cursor over the first image/audio clip and press the space bar, iMovie will play the video. Press the space bar again to stop the playback.

Now record all the other audio scripts and adjust the images to match the audio.

In the viewing screen (upper right) you'll notice the current slide is partially grayed out. iMovie, by default, tries to make the video look sexy by moving the slide viewing area around. To change this and make the slides static, click on the 'fit' button. Do this for each slide.

Play the video several times (use the space bar) and make adjustments as necessary.

When you're satisfied with the video, click on 'file' (in the toolbar) and 'share'. Select 'file' and pick a place to stash the movie on your computer. iMovie will work for a few seconds (or minutes, depending on how long the video is), and the final trailer in mp4 format will be ready for use.

Click on the video and Quicktime Player (anotherMac only program) will open and show the trailer.

Once you have the trailer ready to go, you can upload it to YouTube, embed into your website, and post it online. If you upload it to YouTube, click on the 'share' button and grab the link to the video. Paste the link everywhere so others will find the trailer.

Once the book is published and you have your 'buy links', go back to YouTube and put the links into a comment text box.

My Marketing Plan

To give you a few more insights into book marketing, I'll describe my marketing plan for this book.

Fiction versus non-fiction: First, a few words about the difference between these two types of books. Marketing a novel is quite different from marketing a non-fiction book. With the non-fiction book, you can take a variety of topics in the book and use that material as articles. At the conclusion of each article you add a paragraph that reads: T*he material in this article was taken from my book about {book title}. You can find out more at: {Add book link}*

Fiction, on the other hand, requires more creativity. With my novels, I frequently come up with a tongue-in-cheek interview with my main characters. Excerpts such as scenes are useful also.

My marketing time frame: My marketing efforts began three months before the launch date. Many of the tasks in this book for months 6, 5 and 4 were completed by me long ago and didn't have to be done over.

Amazon Central update: As soon as the book appeared on Amazon as a pre-order, I updated my Amazon Central page. I also update it whenever I receive new material that is appropriate or useful.

Padlet support page: I love Padlet.com. For my book, I created a new page containing support information and downloadable material. I promote the page using the built-in Twitter link and blog posts. The support page can be found here: https://padlet.com/hanque/b0boum9fw405

Trailer: I developed a trailer using the technique described in this chapter. I promote it using Google Ads. The link to the trailer is: https://youtu.be/frFnG6G0BlQ

Lectures: The neat thing about non-fiction books is that you can develop a lecture and take it on tour. For this book, I developed a two-part lecture and plan to give it at a few local libraries. The print book version will be sold at the lectures.

Content articles: I took material from each chapter and developed an article from it. The articles are published on my Medium account:https://medium.com/@hanque99 and on LinkedIn: https://www.linkedin.com/in/hanque/

Blog posts: On my blog post: http://hankquense.org/wp/ I always add a short post about the published articles with a link to the material. This spreads the word abut the articles and the book.

Tweet campaign: In addition to making my own tweets about the book, I tweet about the Padlet support page, the articles and any reviews the book receives.

Booklife promotion: I signed up for a Booklife promotion after I placed the book on the Booklife site

Review requests: I requested early reviews on Goodreads offering Advanced Review Copies to responders. I posted the request on a number of Goodreads groups. I also posted the request in my LinkedIn groups.

Author Marketing Experts blog tour: I signed up for a campaign that includes getting reviews and a blog tour. It's expensive but I think AME is worth the money. Your results may vary.

Booklife contest: I entered the book in Booklife's non-fiction contest.

Compete Index of Tasks

Chapter 1: Getting Started
What type of book?

Comparison List: ebooks & print books
Book titles
Book publishing
Epub3 standard
Book marketing
Budgeting
Publishing budget
Marketing budget

Chapter 2: 6 Months Before Launch
Establish the launch date
Finish the manuscript
Recruit beta readers
Develop a strategic plan

Chapter 3: 5 Months Before Launch
Revise the manuscript
Get a book cover
Create a Goodreads account
Create a Facebook account
Join LinkedIn
Establish a Twitter account
Explore other social media sites

Chapter 4: 4 Months Before Launch
Select packagers
Using packager conversion services
Getting paid
Print on Demand
Hire an editor
Create a web site

Chapter 5: 3 Months Before Launch
Establish the book price
Develop keywords
Write a book blurb
Write a synopsis

Chapter 6: 2 Months Before Launch
Revise the manuscript
Format the book
Complete the book design
Get an ISBN
Upload to packagers
Get advanced review copies
Get a trailer
Create an Amazon Central page
Start social media campaigns
Initiate Goodreads reviewer requests
Start an emil list
Create an email signature
Commission a blog tour

Chapter 7: Launch
Newsletter
Press release
Web announcements
Blog tour sites

Chapter 8: Post-launch
Audio books
Write another book
Get more book reviews
Increase your social media presence
Initiate book campaigns
Organize boo giveaways
Sell physical books

Chapter 9: Your Book Company
Taxes
Revenue splits
Break-even analysis

Chapter 10: Additional Resources
Marketing task prioritization
Support information web page

Checklist
SWOT analysis
Scams
Marketing help
Business help
Fiction book review questionnaire
Non-fiction book questionnaire
Trailer creation
My marketing plan

About the Author

Hank Quense writes humorous and satiric sci-fi and fantasy stories. He also writes and lectures about fiction writing and self-publishing. He has published 19 books and 50 short stories along with dozens of articles. He often lectures on fiction writing and publishing and has a series of guides covering the basics on each subject. He and his wife Pat usually vacation in another galaxy or parallel universe. They also time travel occasionally when Hank is searching for new story ideas.

Other books by Hank Quense

\#

Fiction:

Gundarland Stories

Tales From Gundarland

Falstaff's Big Gamble

Wotan's Dilemma

The King Who Disappeared

Princess Moxie Series

Moxie's Problem

Moxie's Decision

Queen Moxie

Zaftan Troubles Series

Contact

Confusion

Combat

Convolution

Sam

Klatze

Gongeblazn

Non-fiction:

Fiction Writing Workshops for Kids

Business Basics for Authors

Creating Stories

Planning a Novel, Script or Memoir

You can buy any of these books on the websites of all major book sellers.

Links? You want links? Here you go:

Hank's website: http://hankquense.org/wp

Hank's Facebook fiction page:
https://www.facebook.com/StrangeWorldsOnline?ref=hl

Twitter: https://twitter.com/hanque99

LinkedIn: https://www.linkedin.com/in/hanque/

Instagram: https://www.instagram.com/hankquense/

Goodreads: https://www.goodreads.com/author/show/3002079.Hank_Quense

Recently, Hank started a school to share his lectures more widely. The school is run by Udemy.com and you can access a list of his courses at this link: https://www.udemy.com/courses/search/?src=ukw&q=hank%20quense